BETH

by

Julia Scott

Published by New Generation Publishing in 2020

First Edition

ISBN 978-1-80031-578-5

www.newgeneration-publishing.com

 New Generation Publishing

APRIL

Beth sat with her nose pressed against the window as the bus bumped along the potholed road. The window kept steaming up with her breath, it was cold outside; she'd sigh and lean back for a few moments until it cleared, then rest the tip of her nose on the cool pane again. Fat raindrops began to drop from the terminally grey sky, hitting the glass and drizzling lazily downwards carrying Beth's gaze with them. She noticed a sodden, red sock lying in the gutter and, a few metres further on, one large, black canvas shoe, glistening with rain. Whose shoe was it, what was the story behind that sock and shoe, who goes home with one bare foot? A drunk, a homeless person, a mugged illegal immigrant, a road-traffic accident victim? The possibilities were endless.

The top deck of the bus was a must for Beth, quiet and solitary. Downstairs was the place for the compulsive chatterers, those who would pass the time of day with anyone who caught their eye, generally inane topics starting with 'the weather,' all of them totally forgotten within five minutes of stepping off the bus. Beth could never understand the need for idle chit-chat, the compulsion to speak no matter what; no, she was much happier lost in her own thoughts, people watching or thinking about life or about Joe, gentle Joe.

By the time Beth had disembarked ten minutes later the rain was much heavier. Within seconds her dark fringe was plastered to her forehead and a steady flow of raindrops dripped off the tip of her nose. Her denim jacket and black leggings offered little protection against the deluge and her toes were soon squelching inside her skinny trainers. A quick glance at her watch told her she'd have to hurry if she was going to make it to her appointment on time, so she began to run, ducking into the

1

occasional shelter of shop canopies before she reached her destination.

As Beth waited for her name to be called, she noticed the spreading damp patch on the blue fabric of her chair; 'it's going to look as though I've peed myself,' she thought, but surely all the other occupied seats would end up damp too?

"Beth Gregson, Room 4 please," the high-pitched voice jolted her out of her reverie.

The door to room 4 was ajar when Beth found it and she could hear a solitary voice on the other side, clearly one half of a conversation. She gently tapped her knuckles on the door just as she heard the phone land on its cradle.

"Come in Beth, sit down. Now, what can I do for you?"

Doctor Monroe was a large, friendly woman with warm, brown eyes. Soft, dark waves of hair framed her kind face and she smiled as she looked up from her desk; she'd been the Gregson family doctor since before Beth was born, so Beth had neither fear of her nor any sense of embarrassment.

"I'm not sure what's wrong doctor, but something just doesn't feel right. I'm not sleeping well and I'm not so hungry these days, I just feel different, that's all," Beth replied quietly.

"OK. Have you had any headaches or nausea? Any pain anywhere? Have you lost weight? " she asked, with a serious look on her gentle face; Doctor Monroe had always possessed a wonderful blend of friendly concern and professional detachment.

"No, I don't think so," Beth replied after a few moments thought. "I don't weigh myself regularly, but my clothes feel the same as usual, not loose. Actually, they feel a bit tight today, but they're sopping wet from the rain and denim always shrinks when it's wet, doesn't it?"

"Ah, these April showers often catch us out, I know. Ok, let's take a little look at you." Beth sat quietly as her lower eyelids were pulled down, then stood up to have her height and weight checked.

"Mmm, 158cm's and 59kilos, no problem there for a fifteen-year old, sit down again for a moment. How are your periods?"

"Um, well…" Beth whispered, as if confiding a secret, "I'm a late developer. I've only had two periods and they were ok, I think. They both lasted a full week and were a bit heavy, but ok. There was a seven week gap the first time though and it's been ten weeks since the last one, so I don't know what's regular for me yet."

"That's not unusual, they generally take a few months to sort themselves out. Is everything alright at home and school? Nothing's worrying you? Now, I know you're in year eleven, GCSE year, so how's the pressure of study going? Are you coping ok, not feeling overwhelmed at all?"

Beth shook her head and shrugged her shoulders simultaneously, which reassured Kate that there were no obvious signs of stress.

"OK," the doctor said brightly. "I'll ask the nurse to take a blood sample, so we can check a couple of things and we'll test your urine too, just to be thorough. Go and do a tinkle in this jar for me, pop it back into me, then wait in the waiting room for the nurse to call you."

Twenty minutes later, both tasks completed, Beth found herself back in the doctor's surgery.

#

Molly Gregson was lost in thought in Waitrose, opposite the doctor's surgery, in the cake aisle. Her basket was empty apart from a packet of Colombian fresh ground coffee and she simply could not decide on a cake for her reading group ladies later that evening. She was sure she'd seen Beth run into the surgery a short while ago, but she couldn't be sure, after all it was raining hard and the girl who'd so resembled Beth was running with her arm raised, presumably shielding her face from the downpour. But still, it did look like Beth.

Molly decided on her old favourite, a Victoria sponge, then she grabbed a tray of chocolate brownies too, just for good measure. With two pints of milk and a bottle of dry white wine added to her basket she headed for the checkout, hoping for a quick exit so that she could catch the next bus home in five minutes. It was going to be a bit of a rush tonight to get dinner finished with before the reading group ladies arrived, but fortunately Molly had a chicken slow-cooker meal simmering, ready to serve as soon as Beth and Ray were both home. Ray had promised he wouldn't be late tonight, but Molly knew that was a hope rather than a certainty.

Back home in their modern, five-bedroomed detached house, Molly began setting the table for dinner, put dishes to warm in the oven and laid a tea tray for 'her ladies'- best teacups with saucers (no common mugs for Molly) and matching teapot, jug and sugar bowl, plus tea plates and matching serviettes; lastly, the sliced Victoria sponge and brownies were arranged artistically on her best silver platter. White wine already in the fridge to chill, crystal glasses on the sideboard in the living room, the perfect relaxer for the ladies. With a final plumping of the luxuriously soft sofa cushions in the spacious sitting room and a proud 'finger-tipping' of the beautifully crowded vase of roses on the bay windowsill, she was satisfied all was ship-shape for her evening ahead; now she just needed her husband and daughter to be as organised as she was, then all would be well. Where on earth were they both, it was already 5.45pm and not a sign of either of them, typical.

#

Ray Gregson had not had an easy day. Not only had his diary been fully booked from 8.30 am to 5pm, but every single appointment had been monumentally late due to the appalling weather, which meant every single appointment had over-run, which meant he'd had no time for lunch either. Naturally, this was his secretary's fault, stupid girl, but how many times did he have to spell things out to her? Now he was going to be late home too and he'd promised Molly he'd be on time, which meant a moody atmosphere during supper, a perfect end to a perfect bloody day, he thought. He marched over to the antique mahogany coat-stand which adorned one corner of his plush office, grabbed his hat and coat which were still damp from the morning rain and decided to vent his frustration before heading home.

"Sophie, how many times have I explained to you my wet weather timetabling? If it's still wet enough for an umbrella at 9.30am, you cancel the last appointment of both the morning and the afternoon, that way we all have a life," he growled. "It's not rocket science girl, are you deaf, mentally challenged or just plain forgetful?" With that he swept out of the building, slamming the heavy door behind him.

Sophie was not happy; exactly who did he think he was, speaking to her that way? She was a secretary, not a meteorological expert, nor a bouncing board for his furious tempers. For two pins she'd walk out, then he'd see how much he needed her, bad tempered git. She stomped angrily into his office and stared for a few moments at the rain still lashing heavily down the vast sash windows, contemplating her next actions; having composed herself, she tidied his enormous mahogany desk, carried his stale coffee mug to the basin in the corner of the room, then returned to his desk and slid open his bottom drawer. Inside was his precious biscuit tin, full of luxury "only one a day" Belgian chocolate coated biscuits, lid ajar; with her slim, nail-polished fingers, she deftly removed one gorgeous chocolate biscuit and popped it into her mouth whole, savouring its smooth, extravagant taste as it melted slowly on her tongue, then gently crunching the delicate crumb base with her tiny pearly teeth. She expertly dabbed at the corners of her mouth with her fingertips, before delicately removing two more glorious biscuits from the tin and carefully running her tongue along the length of each, then replacing them in their silver cradles, ensuring the lid was left ajar as before.

"That'll teach him to shout at me," she said aloud to herself, then smiled as she closed the drawer and sashayed out of his office on six-inch red heels.

#

Dr Monroe was sitting at her desk and swivelled to face Beth as she entered the room. Beth could not read the expression on the older woman's face, but she knew it was an expression she'd not encountered at the surgery before; it certainly wasn't the relaxed look of twenty minutes earlier.

"Beth, come and sit down, we need to have a chat." Beth did as she was asked, aware of a knot of anxiety creeping into her stomach.

"Beth, tell me, do you have a boyfriend yet?" Now Beth really was puzzled; what sort of question was that and how was it related to her not sleeping well?

"Um well... sort of, not really... but may-be. Joe, he's been my best friend since we were ten, but lately I've started feeling a bit differently about him, like he's more than a friend, if you know what I mean," she stumbled over her words.

"Are you intimate with him," the gentle question came, "do you have physical contact with him?"

"He tickles me sometimes or creeps up and pokes me in the back to surprise me and we have started holding hands sometimes, is that what you mean?" Doctor Monroe leaned forward and looked Beth straight in the eyes with an expression that could only be described as sad.

"Beth sweetie, I've tested your urine and it's telling me that you're pregnant." For a few moments Beth sat stock still, the colour draining out of her face, mouth drooped open, an incredulous look on her face, before she found a weak voice.

"No....what....no....I haven't....we haven't....I've never....we haven't even kissed." The tears began to overflow and trickle down her pale cheeks as she shook her head. "Really, truly, we haven't even kissed, this can't be. How can this be, it's a mistake, you must have made a mistake."

"Beth honey, it's not a mistake and no-one's angry with you, but you must say if someone's forced you to do something you didn't want to do," the tone still kind but firm.

"What? Don't you believe me? I've never done that. Joe is my best friend, he'd never make me do that, he's gentle, what are you saying?"

"Beth, these things happen and we can sort it for you, but right now you're in shock and you need to have some time to think about this and talk to your parents. Would you like me to phone them to come and collect you?"

"No, no, you can't tell them, you mustn't tell them. Do they have to know? They'll be mad with me. I mean, you're not allowed to tell them if I don't want you to, are you?" The tears were now flowing freely down her cheeks, but she was unaware of them until she was handed a tissue.

"You're just fifteen Beth, under-age, they really should know about this. But no, I won't tell them without your permission. Can I call someone else for you, because you have had quite a shock?"

"No, I'll go on the bus. I need to be on my own for a bit. I need to go now, or my mum will wonder where I am."

"OK, but come back and see me first thing in the morning, during the emergency half hour, I'll book you in. And Beth, don't worry, we'll sort this for you." Beth smiled weakly as the door was held open for her, then she quietly left the building and headed for the bus stop, the rain once again beating down on the top of her head.

#

The front door slamming shut brought a frazzled Molly hurriedly out of the kitchen.

"For goodness sake Ray, you said you'd be early tonight; it's already 6.30pm, Beth hasn't got home yet and my ladies are arriving at 7.15pm. Is it really too much to ask, that you heed my requests just once a month? Honestly! I'm dishing up dinner now, Beth will have to have a tray supper in her room" and, with that, Molly stomped back to the kitchen, her high heels clacking on the parquet floor.

"Good evening to you too dear, yes I've had a wonderful day, thank you for asking. Mmm, a lovely supper to match such lovely company, can't wait," he mumbled sarcastically to no-one in particular. Freed from his raincoat, hat and wet shoes, slippered and dry, he wandered into the kitchen and sat at the table where his supper was waiting for him, steaming but somehow not inviting.

"Did you say Beth, isn't home yet? I expect she's sheltering from the rain somewhere with that damn fool Joe. What on earth she sees in that boy I can't imagine; he hasn't said more than half a dozen words to me in the five

8

years we've known him. I sometimes wonder if he isn't a few sheets short of a toilet roll, if you know what I mean."

"You know very well that the phrase is 'a few sandwiches short of a picnic' and he's nothing to worry about, just a bit weak and simple I think. Now hurry up, I'd like dinner cleared and you out of the way before my ladies arrive." Two minutes later, Molly and Ray eating quietly and both privately puzzling over Joe, Beth popped her head around the kitchen door. She was pale, withdrawn and saturated, but neither of her parents really registered this fact, preoccupied as they were with their own thoughts.

"Hi, I'm back. I'm frozen and soaked so I'm going to have a hot shower & get into bed. Not really hungry, I'll get something later if I feel like it. G'night." With that she was gone, her father aware of a very remote twinge of concern, her mother more inclined towards a slightly guilty sense of relief that her evening would not be further disrupted.

#

Joe sat in his tiny bedroom, strumming absent-mindedly on his acoustic guitar. His friend Logan had been given a glossy, red, electric guitar for his sixteenth birthday a few months earlier, but Joe didn't like the tone; he preferred the richer, more mellow sounds of his ancient acoustic, inherited from his great-grandfather who'd received it for his twenty first birthday seventy-five years before. Joe was humming gently and thinking about Beth as he strummed; how strange that she had rushed off after school without speaking to him, when they normally wandered home together, talking over the events of the day. He'd waited in their usual meeting place fifty metres from the school gate, by the post box on the corner, even though it was raining quite heavily; he'd seen her hurry out through the gates and turn in the opposite direction, running to catch the bus which was pulling up beside the kerb further down the road. She'd also switched her mobile off – it had gone straight to voice mail when he'd called. Still, he'd try again later, after supper.

"Joe, come on, fish and chips on the table going cold," his mother bellowed up the narrow staircase. Why on earth she had to shout so loud in this miniscule house when half the volume would have reached him he'd never know. He looked around briefly at the dark green walls he could almost reach out and touch from the middle of the room, the George Ezra poster on the wall opposite his bed, the little window overlooking the street below, the framed photograph on the window ledge of him and Beth in a boat when they were ten, which held his gaze for a few extended moments.

"Coming" he called, then took a deep breath and headed for the stairs.

#

Evening surgery had finished for Kate Monroe. Following Beth's visit she'd had to deal with two patients suffering with nothing more than a heavy cold ('warm drinks, paracetamol if you need it and plenty of walks in the fresh air,') plus one of her regulars, a thirty-five year old hypochondriac who this time was convinced her palpitations indicated heart disease ('switch to decaffeinated tea and coffee and substitute some of your ten cups per day with fruit juice or water'), but Beth was still on her mind. She'd known the Gregson family for sixteen years, since Molly first came to the surgery heavily pregnant with Beth and none too happy about it, one of Kate's first patients after becoming a GP. Beth had always been a fairly robust child, but she'd suffered from mild to moderate asthma and eczema, which meant Kate had seen her annually at the asthma clinic and periodically when her skin flared up. She knew Beth to be a sweet, polite girl, a quiet thinker rather than a boisterous doer, in sharp contrast to either of her parents in Kate's opinion. Molly

Gregson was what Kate called 'a joiner,' – National Childcare Trust, Women's Institute, National Women's Register, Book Club, you name it she joined it; Kate herself had flirted with one or two of these when she was first new to the area, but quickly withdrew due to the pressures of work, evening surgeries and too little time with her husband Wilf. The very few times she'd encountered Ray Gregson at the surgery, always with Beth as he'd insist on seeing a male doctor for himself, she'd found him arrogant, already equipped with a diagnosis for his daughter and capable of writing out a prescription himself, or so he thought, if only it were legal. How they'd managed to produce a lovely girl like Beth was a puzzle to Kate. More to the point, how they were going to respond to Beth's current predicament was a real worry and this was the thought that lingered on Kate's mind as she left the surgery and drove home through the pouring rain to Wilf, a painful reminder that it was a problem they'd never face themselves, having survived five long years of IVF treatment unsuccessfully.

#

The dial in the shower read 37° C, not nearly hot enough for Beth, so she turned it up to 40° C; with the excessively hot water beating down on her bare shoulders, she was quickly cocooned in her own, private, steamy world, but nothing could stop her thawing body from shaking violently. She was trapped in a world of desperate denial, trapped by her own body. She was in shock, in total disbelief. Time seemed to be lost, she could have been standing there for five minutes or five hours, she didn't know. Eventually she switched off the shower, wrapped herself in her thick, pink towelling bathrobe and climbed into bed, pulling the duvet up over her head, which is how she remained for most of the night, eyes wide open, trying to understand what was happening.

The black clouds weighed heavily on Kate as she drove home and her spirits plummeted a little further with each passing grey mile. As she pulled up into her drive and climbed out of her car, the automatic outside light flicked on, brightening the front of the house to a level way above her weary heart.

She could hear soft music coming from the kitchen as she closed the front door behind her and she could smell something meaty and delicious leaking from the warm kitchen atmosphere. Wilf came out to meet her with his normal bear hug, today somehow gentler than usual – he was so sensitive to her mood changes, he could read her like a book.

"Tough day?" he asked, as he kissed her forehead.

"Some of it was," she replied, as she buried her face in his chest.

"Want to talk about it?" he coaxed.

"No, I can't right now, may-be later."

"OK. How about you relax in a lovely warm bath before supper? You go and get into your robe while I run it for you. Supper and a glass of wine will be ready and waiting for you in thirty minutes, OK?"

"Fine, thanks, you're a love."

However, as Kate reached the top of the stairs, she did not go into their room to change; instead she went quietly into the would-be-nursery-now-overflow room next door. She knelt on the floor in front of the pristine white chest with pastel green and yellow knobs and tenderly opened the bottom drawer. She first lifted out the tiny, soft, white cotton vest and held it to her cheek, then the pale-yellow shawl which she held to her nose, inhaling the intoxicating smell of baby-soft soapflakes. As usual, she thought her heart would break, but no tears escaped her eyes; she was way beyond tears, still swamped by raw grief as she thought back.

She remembered being not much older than Beth, almost seventeen, when her life changed so very much, yet so little. She remembered the party at her best friend Megan's house, every room heaving with people from her year at school. She remembered hearing that alcohol had been smuggled in against parental rules, remembered the several large tumblers of orange juice, heavily laced with anonymous vodka, so funny at first. She remembered the sense of the lost few hours which followed, the panic, the questions which she could not answer. She remembered waking to find herself on a bedroom floor, skirt around her waist, tights and knickers in a dishevelled heap nearby and blood, definitely blood and discomfort.

Kate also remembered the agony of realising her period was late, of being in denial just like Beth, of later becoming aware of the first butterfly fluttering movements of the life growing inside her. Then her parents, forcing her into an almost-too-late abortion, putting her studies and prospective life in medicine ahead of all else.

"You have your whole life ahead of you Kate, don't mess it up now. Plenty of time for babies later," they said. Famous last words, Kate had bitterly come to realise. Was she subsequently punished for this termination early in her life? If she had known then that she had been facing her only chance at motherhood, would she have accepted her parent's words or would she have fought harder? Was God teaching her a lesson? As always, questions, questions, but no answers.

She solemnly replaced the baby things in their lifeless storage and quietly left the room. Wilf came out of the bathroom a moment before she disappeared into their bedroom, then tiptoed down the stairs, knowing he was powerless to help her.

#

By 6am the next morning Beth had come to the one possible conclusion, convinced that Dr Monroe had made a monumental mistake, possibly after an exhausting day at the surgery and had mixed up Beth's pee with someone else's. The other pee sample could even belong to some poor woman trying desperately to become pregnant, who'd gone home miserable because she'd been told her test had been negative. Yes, that had to be it.

With renewed enthusiasm despite feeling drained, Beth got ready for school early, bundled her tangled black hair into a messy ponytail and crept downstairs, relieved to find that neither of her parents had yet made an appearance in the kitchen. She quickly and quietly helped herself to a glass of cold milk, glugging it down in ten seconds flat, grabbed an apple from the fruit bowl on the table and tiptoed out of the house, encouraged to discover that the day was dry and promised to be sunny by the look of the muted shadows cast by the trees on the pavement. She decided to walk the two miles to the surgery, partly to liven herself up and partly to make sure she was there when Dr Monroe arrived, ready to reassure her that all was ok, anyone could make a mistake, no ill feelings. By the time she was half way to the surgery Beth was feeling far more positive, almost normal and ready for the day ahead and, for the first time in over twelve hours, she thought about Joe; poor Joe, he must have got soaked waiting for her yesterday and he'd probably be annoyed that she hadn't called him. Never mind, she'd tell him all about it later, on the way home after school, they'd probably have a really good laugh about it. With almost a bounce in her step she headed for the surgery, mentally preparing what she would say to Kate Monroe.

#

Beth was not the only one who'd had a wakeful night; Kate had awakened several times, worried that Beth might have done something silly and out of character, eventually forcing herself back into a fitful sleep. Joe had also struggled with sleeplessness, instinctively knowing there was something bad going on with Beth, that she was in some sort of trouble, but why hadn't she phoned him? He was her closest friend wasn't he, closer even than her parents, *especially* her parents? Why would she not share her problems now, when she always had done so in the past? He had sensed their relationship was changing, growing closer over the past few months, but may-be she'd didn't feel the same, may-be he shouldn't have started holding her hand when they walked home each day, but it felt so good, so right, so natural. He resolved to get to school early and wait by the post box again, then he'd see her arriving and hopefully grab a few moments with her to check all was ok before going into class.

#

Kate Monroe also made an early start that day and she was surprised to see Beth sitting on the steps of the surgery as she drove her car in through the permanently open gates. She took her time parking in the bay reserved for her, trying to decide how best to approach this situation.

"Hello Beth, my goodness you're here early, we're not due to open for another hour. Come on in and I'll make us both a cuppa, I can't function without at least two cups."

Not another word was spoken as the two of them entered through the large blue doors and walked through the bright, modern, enormous waiting room and on into the surprisingly small kitchen at the rear of the building. Beth sat on the only stool; Kate boiled the kettle and popped two teabags into two mugs, poured on the water, reached into the small fridge for milk and finally removed the tea bags, all the while saying nothing, trying to assess Beth's mood. As it turned out, Beth was the one to break the silence.

"I've been awake all night and I've come to the only possible explanation. That is, you've mixed up my pee with someone else's. Don't worry, I'm not angry and my parents don't know, so my dad won't come and rant at you, anyone could make a mistake. But that has to be it, I'm sure."

"OK, let's go through to my room and talk. Bring your tea, would you like a biscuit too?" Beth shook her head. Kate would have to tread lightly, she could see that, classic denial, not surprising really. They each sipped their tea for a few minutes, quiet with their own thoughts, sitting in the unnecessary privacy of Kate's room. Where to begin Kate wasn't sure, but begin she must, gently.

"Beth, you're no doubt tired if you've been awake all night, that's perfectly understandable, but I want you to stay calm for me. Beth, yours was the only pee sample in my room last night, truly, so there couldn't be a mistake. But if you like we can test another sample, just to be sure, how about that?"

"No, no need, you made a mistake I'm sure. I've never had sex so I can't be pregnant, simple. May-be the blood test will show I'm anaemic or something, but I'll just wait for my next period and then you'll see I'm not pregnant. Will you call me if there's anything wrong with my blood?" The tone was anxious but determined; Kate could see that she'd have to try a different approach.

"How about you come back and see me in two weeks if your period hasn't come by then? If the blood test shows up anything the results can be posted or I'm sure I have your mobile number on record, but I really don't expect it to."

"No, no post and no mobile, I'll call the surgery," Beth stated emphatically.

"Ok, but in the meantime, you call me if you need to talk about anything. As I said yesterday, we can sort this out, so don't start worrying too much, ok?" Beth nodded, placed half a cup of tea on Kate's desk and left without saying another word. Kate flicked through fourteen pages in her diary and wrote in capitals at the top of the page: 'NB: Pt 2601? HCG,' which was medical code for 'Beth Gregson, pregnant?' then she headed for the kitchen to make herself a fresh cup of tea.

#

Joe sat at the kitchen table opposite his little brother Freddy, whilst his mother placed a plate of bacon and eggs in front of each of them, then sat down with a third plate for herself. Joe watched as Freddy swamped his breakfast with tomato ketchup then began to devour it noisily. Joe stared at the mop of unruly, unbrushed morning hair, so like his own, so dark and wavy. He wondered at the ten-year old's concentration, totally focused on the task in front of him.

"I don't know why mum bothers to cook for you; if she placed two socks and a bar of soap on your plate it would still taste the same, just ketchup! You wouldn't even notice!" Joe watched him for a moment longer, then tucked into his own breakfast, remembering his plan to reach school early to wait for Beth.

"Don't start on him Joe," Martha Lehman interrupted, "let's have a nice peaceful breakfast together please.

Freddy, try to eat more quietly." Twenty minutes later both boys had left for school, Freddy annoyed that he'd had to rush his breakfast in order to go early with Joe, Joe exasperated that he'd had to wait for Freddy and was now later than he'd hoped – if Beth was early too, he might have already missed her. Joe frog-marched a moaning Freddy the half mile to his school and watched briefly as his brother showed an uncharacteristic burst of energy and ran to his mates in the already noisy playground, then Joe sprinted the final half mile to his own school and waited hopefully by the post box for Beth.

Meanwhile, Martha Lehman pulled on her leopard print rubber gloves with a fur collar and began to wash the remnants of cold egg yolk and bacon grease off the breakfast plates with lukewarm water – blast that old boiler, she'd forgotten to ask Jack if she could order a new one, she'd have to boil a kettle to finish the washing up now. As she stood waiting for the kettle to boil Martha wondered where Jack was, she never knew exactly. She could picture him in the cab of his five-tonne lorry well enough, but beyond that, she could never imagine the towns or countryside he was travelling through at any given time; truth was, she'd long ago given up even trying. She had grown accustomed to their marriage pattern, Jack away for two weeks at a time, only home every other weekend; it suited her, suited her need for freedom, no need to consult with anyone about where she went or what she did, as long as she was there for her two boys. Alternate weekends at home suited Jack too; it was long enough to catch up with his two boys, long enough to enjoy a few home cooked meals, long enough to sort out any small jobs pending in the house, long enough for a couple of urgent fumbling sessions beneath the duvet with Martha, long enough to do his duty all round, before the blissful release of driving off in his lorry on a Monday morning for another two weeks traversing the continent, delivering best quality British oak timber to factories in

Eastern Europe. He loved it, the freedom, the lack of responsibility, as long as his conscience was clear that Martha and the boys had been catered for.

An added bonus for Martha was that, with Jack away, she could pursue her Christian convictions without any argument from him. Throughout seventeen years of marriage he'd remained impervious to her faith, detached, immune and occasionally downright 'anti.' In the early years she'd tried to explain it to him numerous times, tried to share it with him, believing he would value his life so much more if he could tune into the transience of it, the briefness of existence, the belief that there was more beyond the grave, but he resisted manfully. Each time she'd tried, she was aware of the spaces behind his eyes and his heart closing like lift doors, blocking her and her faith out.

'*Religion is just a crutch for the weak,*' he'd say. '*It's caused more wars and more deaths than all the plagues, famines, droughts, floods, tsunamis and earthquakes put together. Open your eyes woman and think for yourself for once. And if you think I'm spending an hour in church every other Sunday, when I only get two days off a fortnight, you've got another think coming.*' None of this had affected Martha's convictions though, it just made her keep her faith low-key when Jack was home and satisfyingly open when he was away. She'd go around the house with a small box the day before he was due home, collecting up her crucifix from above the front door, her rosary beads from around the lamp in the living room and her statue of Our Lady from the shelf in the kitchen, replacing them every other Monday morning.

Washing up completed, she set about peeling potatoes and organising dinner in advance, knowing that she had a meeting at St Thomas' later that evening. As she placed a speedily assembled cottage pie in the fridge the clock on the Welsh dresser clicked into action – a little gilt door opened to reveal a smiling Jesus, accompanied by an instrumental burst of Ave Maria before a tiny bell chimed ten times. The clock had been a wedding present from Sister Cecilia, Martha's old headmistress from St Bernadette's High School for Girls and remained the one Catholic artefact Joe had tolerated for seventeen years, the one item never put away prior to his homecomings.

#

As Beth had almost an hour to spare between leaving Kate Monroe's surgery and school starting, she decided to slowly walk the mile journey and enjoy the increasingly bright morning. She needed to think, to understand why a doctor wouldn't admit a simple mistake, to clear her mind of the ridiculous notion that she could be pregnant when she was still a virgin. Not remotely possible, she was adamant, a conclusion she had managed to convince herself of by the time she noticed Joe waiting by the post box.

"Hello you, everything ok?" he asked as she approached.

"Yeah, sorry about yesterday, I had a doctor's appointment and had to rush; forgot to turn my phone back on."

"Is anything wrong, going to the doctor's I mean?"

"Nah, just girl stuff, don't want to discuss it really. Meet me by the post box later, ok? Better go in or we'll be late." They walked in through the massive plain, grey, iron gates towards the wide stone steps leading up to the main school entrance, but Joe noticed how distracted Beth was, despite her smiling best efforts to hide it. Something was wrong, he was sure, but if it was "girl stuff" may-be he shouldn't ask.

Later that day, waiting by the post box for Beth again, Joe saw her coming back down the school steps with her arms full of books, which she'd collected at lunchtime, deliberately so that her hands would not be free to hold either of his. She knew that he knew that it was unnecessary to carry books when every subject was freely available on the internet, but she couldn't think of another way to avoid touching him and avoiding physical contact with him was vital to her today, but she didn't know why.

"What's with all the books, want me to carry some?" he asked kindly, puzzled though he was.

"Nah, it's ok, they're cookery books, I want to be better at cooking," she replied too quickly; but Joe knew she wasn't remotely interested in cookery, never had been, not even as a little kid when it involved melting chocolate to make rice crispy cakes. He became more and more puzzled as they walked silently down the road towards home.

#

Apart from the occasional bright morning, the second half of April continued to be cold and blustery with heavy showers and even a few snow flurries, which did nothing to lighten Beth's load or ease her hidden worries. She needed sunshine, warmth, escape. Despite her best efforts to ignore her sore, swollen breasts and the infuriating nausea which had begun to plague her throughout the days, she was acutely aware that her period still had not arrived and that she would have to return to the surgery; there had been no letter or text message from the doctor with blood test results, but Beth remained convinced she merely had anaemia or something, so a return visit to collect some iron tablets or similar seemed inevitable. On the other hand, perhaps if she just ignored the situation the doctor would forget all about it too and life could return to normal – she'd think about it for a few more days.

At least school, boring though it had become, was a distraction from the constant nausea and the niggling worry over her advancing bodily symptoms. PSHCE next on relationships, with 'Fatkins' herself, very tall, overweight Mrs Adkins with short, wispy grey hair – no way did she know anything at all about relationships in the twenty first century, with her voluminous gathered skirts down past her knees, masculine lace-up shoes and bare legs that hadn't seen a razor in over thirty years, Beth mused.

"Right, Year 11, settle down now and switch off your mobiles please, we'll begin in one minute exactly," came the booming voice which made all three chins wobble comically. As 'Fatkins' loaded a DVD into the class computer, thirty pupils rapidly switched their mobiles to silent mode, as the concept of *actually turning them off* was, naturally, totally unacceptable – was she completely insane?

The next hour and a half was something of a shock to Beth's sensitivities, though she did her very best to appear bored and blasé about the information crowding in on her brain and to ignore the sniggering and wise cracks made by some of her immature classmates. By the end of the session she knew all there was to know about heterosexual sex, homosexual sex, lesbian sex and masturbation, as well as the surprising revelation that experimenting with all of these was not only normal, healthy and socially acceptable, but was also to be welcomed. She also now had detailed knowledge of methods to avoid pregnancy, from female condoms, six-monthly injections, IUD's and 'morning after' pills to the huge variety of male condoms available, one of which she'd had to practise unrolling on to a banana. This, of course, had been the most excruciatingly embarrassing activity for Beth, but one of great hilarity for the class clowns.

With two minutes left before the end of the session, 'Fatkins' had left a pathetically small window of opportunity for questions, but it appeared that either everyone was too embarrassed to ask anything or that they were already fully knowledgeable in the world of sex. Only one solitary voice was heard and Beth was surprised to see that it was Joe's.

"Excuse me Mrs Adkins, but an hour and a half ago you said we'd be discussing relationships, but I haven't heard anything about what happens before you get to the point of having sex. I haven't heard about feelings, about respect or about caring for the person you're supposed to have sex with. Shouldn't those things be considered too?" Joe's words were almost drowned out by the boos and groans of numerous morons, but Beth felt a surge of something very strong and unidentifiable for him and she watched anxiously as he ignored the noise around him and waited for an answer.

"Joe, you can have relationships without sex and you can have sex without relationships, but we really don't have time to go into this now. Perhaps we'll discuss it another time." The lame response was clearly inadequate and Mrs Adkins was uncomfortable, knowing that she was not going to escape so easily.

"Exactly, sex and relationships are two separate things and you have only talked about sex, so what about relationships?" Joe felt he deserved an answer.

"Another time Joe, another time," then 'Fatkins' left the classroom without meeting his eyes. Beth watched her leave, pushing and elbowing her way through the muddle of students squeezing through the door, then she stood for a few moments, trying to understand her own muddled emotions.

Joe was not satisfied and remained in his seat staring blankly at the bowl of condom-clad bananas on the front table, feeling strangely sad and empty. Aware suddenly that Beth was watching him he quickly stood up and packed his bag.

"What a waste of an hour and a half and what a shocking bloody waste of bananas," he said, "do you think they're still fit to eat? I could take some home to mum." Beth felt a grin spread across her face.

"I think your mum might be unhappy with them as they are and I also think they might be rather bruised by the time you get the condoms back off, don't you? Come on, let's go home. I've got a virgin banana in my bag if you're hungry." They were both still grinning as they walked out through the school gates together.

MAY

On 3rd May Kate drove to her morning surgery in bright sunshine, the weather having finally taken a turn for the better. Suddenly there were daffodils appearing in the grass banks along the lanes, magnolia buds making a first colourful appearance on bleak, dry branches and the first bursts of blossom on so many trees, at last a suggestion that summer might be on the way.

Once in her surgery and with a strong, dark cup of tea on her desk, Kate flicked open her diary and instantly noticed the bold letters at the top of the page: 'NB: Pt 2061?HCG'

"Oh dear," she said aloud to herself, "come on Kate, sort it out." A quick glance at the clock on the wall told her it was 8.15am and a reasonable time to call Beth's mobile – late enough for the family to be up and about, not so late that they'd all have left to start their days; she knew this was professionally dodgy, but Beth had failed to contact her and so gave her little choice – she picked up the phone.

Beth had left early for school, partly to meet Joe and partly to avoid seeing her mum and facing the inevitable nag session, but she'd caught her arm on the door handle in the hallway and dropped her schoolbag, emptying the contents all over the floor. She was so sure that the noise would alert her parents that she'd stuffed everything rapidly back in and darted out the front door, not realising her mobile was still on the floor under the hall table.

Molly Gregson was coming down the stairs and heard the phone buzzing, not sure where it was coming from. She saw it under the table and bent to pick it up, simultaneously smudging the newly applied red nail polish on her thumb as she pressed the answer button.

"Damn and blast" was all Kate heard initially, then "Oh sorry, Molly Gregson here, who's calling?"

"Hello Mrs Gregson, it's Dr Monroe here, I thought I was calling Beth, could I please speak to her?"

"No, I'm sorry, she's already left for school and forgotten her phone, can I help you?"

"I need to speak to her about the results of some tests I did for her, could you please ask her to call the surgery and make an appointment?"

"Can't you just tell me, I am her mother after all?"

"I'm sorry Mrs Gregson, I have to respect patient confidentiality despite Beth's tender age. If you could just ask her to make an appointment with me soon, thank you," Kate replied as gently as she could.

"I'm sorry no, that's not really good enough. Beth's only fifteen and I'm her mother, I have a right to know if my daughter is ill, don't I?", came the somewhat shrill response.

"Actually no, you don't, not unless Beth wishes to tell you herself. Now if you'll excuse me, I must prepare myself for morning surgery. Good morning to you," then she replaced the phone in its cradle as she took a deep breath. Kate was instantly unhappy that she may have added to Beth's problems by calling, but really she'd had no alternative as Beth had failed to make contact herself. 'Oh well, every action has a reaction and Beth needs a prompt,' Kate mused to herself as she reviewed her patient list for the morning surgery.

Molly Gregson, however, was extremely miffed. How dare that woman refuse to discuss her underage child with her and how could Beth make her own mother look such a fool by not telling her what was going on? Some firm talking was required, Molly could see that, just as soon as Beth got home. Angrily preoccupied for a few minutes with an imagined conversation with Beth later in the day, Molly's train of thought was interrupted by the home phone ringing, which she snatched up immediately.

"What?" she almost shouted into the receiver.

"Whoa, what's annoyed you so early in the day?" Ray questioned as he rubbed his smarting ear.

"It's that bloody woman at the surgery, Kate Monroe. She refuses to tell me why Beth went to see her, refuses to discuss *'confidential test results'* as she called them; Beth's fifteen, for goodness sake, I have a right to know and I can't believe Beth put me in this position."

"Well, don't do your normal thing of over-reacting, I'm sure Beth will tell you what's going on. I just hope she's not letting that damn fool Joe pressurise her into going on the pill or anything. Anyway, more importantly, I forgot to tell you that Finn Orlandsen is coming back with me tonight and he'll be staying for a couple of nights, so we'll be four for dinner, OK?" Molly did not like her routines altered, especially at short notice and it was not unusual for Ray to spring things on her like this. In Molly's opinion it showed a lack of consideration towards her, taking her for granted, just because she was a housewife with no independent earnings.

"Why is he coming again? It's only a couple of weeks since he was here before, can't he stay in a guest house or something?" Ray tried to remain calm, he didn't want to annoy Molly further, he wanted her in a pleasant mood if they had a guest for dinner.

"I'm sorry this is short notice, but it's actually eleven weeks since he last visited and you know he's a valued part of this business Molly. I need a partner in Switzerland and he's turning out to be a good one, so please make him welcome even if you don't feel like it. I'm sending a car to pick him up from the airport at 3pm and bring him back to the office, so we'll both be home by 6pm, OK? After dinner we'll be in the study going over paperwork, so your whole evening won't be swallowed up, you'll have time to talk to Beth quietly."

Conversation over, Molly began planning the evening's menu, but she remained annoyed at both Ray and Beth in equal measure. Within twenty minutes she was back on the bus heading towards Waitrose again, wondering if either of them realised how lucky they were to have her.

Ray knew that Molly was annoyed with him; he knew that he should have told her of Finn's visit days before, knew that he should be more considerate of her. More importantly, he also knew that her annoyance with him would burn itself out and that she would soon switch into professional hostess mode, such was her pride in her home and her obsession with always making a good impression. Her social skills were second to none and an asset to him, he was well-aware, confident that she would put on a convincing show of liking Finn, even though she had instinctively disliked him when he'd entered their home previously. Confident that all would be fine at home later, Ray dragged his thoughts back to the clinic and the reason Finn was currently on a plane headed towards him. He pressed his thumb firmly on the intercom on his desk.

"Sophie, did you remember to order a car to pick up Mr Orlandson from Bristol at 3pm today?"

"Yes Mr Gregson, all sorted yesterday," she replied instantly. "Shit, shit, shit!" was what the customers in the waiting room heard immediately she had switched off her intercom. She looked up to see four pairs of eyes staring at her intently, waiting for her next move, which involved calmly extracting an emery board from her top drawer to smooth an imaginary rough edge on one of her immaculate, elegantly red fingernails. Damn it, she'd blame the taxi firm for not turning up, no-one would ever know.

#

Molly was in the kitchen when Beth arrived home from school. No sooner had Beth stepped through the door than she was overwhelmed by the strong aroma of vegetable soup, which immediately made her retch. She swallowed forcefully and tried to calm herself as her mother called her into the kitchen, where she was artistically piping double cream on to some elaborate desert. Beth almost retched again at the sight.

"How nice to have you home at a normal time for once, no Joe tonight?" The tinge of sarcasm in Molly's voice was not lost on Beth.

"No, Joe had to go straight home for an early dinner because his mum's out tonight. I'm going over to his later to babysit Freddy with him."

"Well we've got company tonight so you may not be free early enough to go out again. Your father's arranged for Finn Orlandsen to stay for a couple of nights so we won't be eating until 7pm at the earliest; he said they'd be here by 6pm, but we all know that we can add at least an hour on to that."

"I don't like that man, he's creepy, why can't he stay in a hotel? Can't I have a tray supper upstairs and then go to Joe's?"

"No, he's your father's partner or associate or something and we must make him feel welcome by sharing a meal together; they'll be in the study for most of the evening anyway," Molly said as she popped the desert into the fridge and turned to face Beth. Her expression was thunderous and she was clearly struggling to keep her annoyance under control. "Dr Monroe called you this morning just after you'd left; she wanted to discuss some test results and she refused point blank to discuss them with me. Can you imagine, your own mother not being allowed to know what's going on with her own daughter? The blasted woman was so rude and I felt like an idiot, so thank you for putting me in *that* position. So, what's going on, what tests does she mean?" Molly's stare made Beth uncomfortable and she was aware of a combined feeling of anxiety and relief rolled into one – thank goodness Kate Monroe hadn't discussed the details. Beth tried hard to keep her face from betraying her emotions and meant to sound calm as she opened the fridge for fruit juice, but her voice was strangely tight as she replied.

"Oh, I was feeling really tired all the time and I thought I might be anaemic or something, so I went to see her a few weeks ago. I don't want to be ill with the exams coming up and everything." She poured herself a small glass of juice and returned the carton to the fridge, painfully aware that her mother's glare was boring into her like a knife.

"Well she wants you to call her. I don't appreciate being made to look a fool Beth, you should have told me you were going to see her."

"Mum I'm fifteen not five, I don't need to tell you every last detail, I'm allowed some privacy. I'm going to change, I'll call her from upstairs." Beth left the kitchen to escape both her mother and the smell of vegetables, which were beginning to make her feel distinctly queasy. As she headed upstairs she was confronted by all the fears she had tried so hard to block out of her thoughts for the last few weeks, but she knew she would not call Kate Monroe from upstairs, it would have to be her mobile later, much later.

#

Martha Lehman placed a steaming bowl of beef stew in the centre of the weathered pine table, next to a basket of bread rolls, just as Joe and Freddy walked into the cosy kitchen and sat down. Joe looked at her intently, thinking how lucky he was to have a mum who cared about them so much, compared to Beth's mum who always seemed so remote and unfriendly. Beth's mum may be tall, elegant, blonde and artificially perfect whilst Martha was small, softer with shoulder-length thick hair which had a mind of its own, but he wouldn't swap for anything.

"What's that look for, do I have stew splashes on my face or something?" she asked as a smile spread across her face.

"No, no, just appreciate you, that's all," Joe said as he smiled back. "Where's your meeting tonight mum?"

"Back at St Thomas' hall again, but I won't be late tonight, should be back by 9.30pm."

"Why do you go to so many meetings mum, why so many committees?" Freddy didn't like her going out, for him home felt better when she was in it.

"Well someone has to care about things beyond their own existence, don't they? Where would we be if we all stayed wrapped up in our own little lives and didn't care about the rest of the world?" She dropped a kiss on Freddy's messy head as she placed a bowl in front of him.

"What is it tonight mum, should I know about it?" Joe was so like Martha, so caring and concerned about social issues. He may be tall and slim like his dad, but his personality was hers through and through.

"It's a pro-life meeting Joe; we're going to discuss the possibility of having silent prayer vigils outside the hospital on some days when certain 'procedures' are taking place. We can't do much more for the lives being harmed or the poor little souls lost on those days."

"What are 'procedures' mum?" Freddy chirped in, not wanting to be left out of the conversation.

"It's when certain medical things are done to people Freddy; sometimes procedures are necessary to make sick people well again, but sometimes these procedures are not necessary and are just done for convenience, but they hurt other people, so we don't think it's right to do that." Martha knew she was being vague, but she was not happy to worry a ten-year-old with unpleasant facts.

"I don't understand mum; why would a doctor do anything to hurt someone? I thought doctors and hospitals were there to help people, so no wonder people are scared when they have to go there. I'm never going there, ever!"

"No love, the doctors don't mean to hurt anyone. The people who have these procedures mostly *choose* to have them; they don't know it could hurt them badly until afterwards. Now eat up your stew and stop worrying about it because it will never happen to you."

Freddy started spooning delicious stew into his mouth, quietly thinking he'd have to be more careful when he played football if he didn't want to go to the hospital for a 'procedure.' Martha watched him, knowing he was pondering on her clearly unsatisfactory explanation, but she was at a loss as to how she could have made it clearer whilst protecting his innocence.

#

It was almost 8pm before Finn followed Ray into his study for the remainder of the evening. The agenda was private, not for the ears of Molly or Beth; in fact, Molly had always remained totally uninterested in the true nature of Finn's activities as Ray's partner. Finn was tall, fair, classically handsome and extremely well groomed, but there was something about him that made both Molly and Beth go cold inside.

"Ray, the problem is that we need more merchandise from you, more regular deliveries to Switzerland. The clinic in Berne needs a constant supply to continue the research; we can't have scientists sitting around waiting for products to use, it's too costly. We're paying top dollar for high quality goods, but supply is falling short of demand right now, so we need to come up with some strategies to increase supply. I'm only here for a few days, so I need to sit in on your consultations, watch how you handle clients and so on. It's possible we'll have to compromise on the quality in favour of quantity, if you know what I mean."

"I hear what you're saying Finn, but quality is important. Surely the research can't be dependable if the products are not as pure as possible? My clinic has only been in operation for two years and it takes time to build confidence, get a name for yourself, you must realise that?"

"I do Ray, but you must see our predicament too. You want a slice of the rewards when our research is available world-wide; you want your name and your clinic to be acknowledged features of our success. In order for that to happen we need to stay with you, not look elsewhere for

British partners, so you need to meet our demands, simple as that."

"Ok Finn, spend the next couple of days with me at the clinic, give me some input here. We can sort this, now how about a drink?"

#

Joe opened his front door moments before Beth rang the bell, which took her by surprise.

"I saw you through the window sorry, didn't mean to make you jump."

"No prob's, I'm just relieved to be here 'cos dad's loathsome partner is stopping with us and he gives me the shivers. Really, I can't stand the man; so what are we doing tonight, I need my mind taking off him?"

"Freddy's up for another hour so I told him we'd play Wii tennis, his favourite, then we'll watch a film or something. Mum said she'd give you a lift home later, so you'll be tucked up in bed by midnight, ok?"

"Great, let's get started. Got any nibbles 'cos I'm starving? I couldn't eat with that awful man watching me."

"Homemade flapjacks, popcorn and giant chocolate cookies should do the trick. Freddy, load up, we're ready to play." Just over an hour later Freddy was up in his room and Beth was sitting at the pine table in the kitchen while Joe made hot chocolate for them all. Beth looked around at the Welsh dresser filled with mis-matched mugs, tea plates and jugs, at the draining boards full of still damp dinner plates and glass tumblers (obviously no dishwasher would fit in) and at the threadbare hand-towel hanging on the doorknob, yet she could feel the warmth and love of a close family in this tiny, worn kitchen, a warmth strangely lacking in her own spacious, tidy, spotless kitchen at home. What was it that made the difference other than money, she wondered? She pondered this for a few moments, but could not come up with a satisfying answer.

"So, where's your mum gone tonight, somewhere exciting?"

"Nah, just one of her committee meetings. It's a pro-life group and you should have heard her trying to explain it to Freddy this morning, I think she's put him off hospitals for ever;" he began to laugh so loudly at the memory that he spilled the hot chocolate he was holding all over the floor. "Shit, can you make another one while I mop this up, then we'll start the film." Beth reached a fresh mug down from the dresser and filled it with milk before placing it in the microwave.

"Pro-life, what's that exactly?"

"Um, I don't know the full story, but I think they're against euthanasia and abortion and anything that forces an unnatural end to life. I really admire her strength, 'cos it's not easy to hold unpopular views and stand up for them. They're planning to stand outside the hospital on abortion days, holding up posters with information about alternatives to passers by. I hope she doesn't get punched or anything when she's protesting in this way. Don't slip on the damp patch now will you," he said as he washed his hands.

Beth said nothing for a few moments as she absent-mindedly stirred milk into the cocoa, becoming aware of a sudden knot of anxiety in her stomach as she was reminded indirectly of her possible predicament.

"Come on," she said more gruffly than she intended and making Joe look at her in surprise, "are we watching this film or what?"

"Yep, I'll just take Freddy his cocoa and you can take ours through, if that's ok with you. Press 'start,' I'll be back before you know it."

#

As Molly drove Beth home some time later, she wondered why Beth was so uncommunicative.

"You OK? You're very quiet tonight, good film?"

"Yep, fine and fine, I'm just tired." And with that Beth rested her head against the window and feigned sleep, putting an end to further conversation. Fifteen minutes later, she was in her own bedroom, sitting naked on the edge of her bed, looking at her swollen, painful breasts. Though her stomach was still flat, she could no longer deny the other changes in her body, but she still could not accept that she might be pregnant. How could she be, when she had never had intercourse? Pondering this problem over and over was exhausting, until a sudden thought occurred to her. Hormones. She must have a hormone imbalance, that was it. Why on earth didn't she think of it before and, more to the point, why hadn't Dr Monroe spotted it? Could a hormone imbalance cause a false pregnancy reading? It must do, it really must do. With her heart and her head both full of renewed hope, Beth was suddenly overwhelmed with a searing pain in her lower belly and a desperate urge to go to the toilet, where she was soon shocked by the blood stains on the toilet tissue. Her period, at last, what a painful relief.

#

The following day at the surgery was a hectic one for Kate Monroe because one of her colleagues was ill, meaning she'd had to cover a number of his appointments as well as her own. She'd had no lunch break and only two cold cups of coffee all day, so it was a blessed relief to see the final patient leave at 6.30pm. She was just shutting down her computer when there was a knock on her door as it gently opened, followed by a very apologetic request by the practice nurse asking if Kate would speak to Beth Gregson, who had just walked into the surgery. Kate momentarily buried her face in her hands and took a huge breath, then smiled and asked for Beth to be shown in.

"Come in Beth, I was hoping you'd contact me. Did your mother pass on my message to you?"

"Yes, she did. I just wanted to tell you that my period arrived, so there's no need to worry now. I must have a hormone imbalance or something, but it's ok now."

"Well Beth, it's certainly possible that a hormone imbalance would delay the onset of your periods and even hinder them becoming regular, but it wouldn't be responsible for a false pregnancy reading. Shall we maybe repeat the pee sample and blood test to be sure? Perhaps I could examine you?"

"No!" The firm response was unmistakeable. "There's no need, I'm not pregnant, my period arrived, I told you. I just wanted to let you know. I have to go now, bye." And with that Beth was gone. Kate took another deep breath and suddenly noticed how exhausted she felt. She wondered what was really going on in Beth's mind; was it possible that Beth, noticing some blood loss, had accepted it as her period and consequently convinced herself that she was not pregnant, when she could actually be in danger of a miscarriage, or was the poor girl just terrified? And why did she, Kate, feel so involved, when she'd dealt many times over the years with unwanted teenage pregnancies? The answer, of course, was because Beth was adamant that she was still a virgin, so the liklihood of abuse or a date rape was entirely possible and it was too close to home for Kate. Some scars never heal. All Kate knew for sure was that this story was far from over.

#

Sophie was just taking off her coat when Ray Gregson and Finn Orlandson walked in through the main doors to the clinic.

"Two coffees Sophie, both black and no sugar, straight away."

"Right," she replied as they disappeared into Ray's office and shut the door. *'Please Sophie'* wouldn't kill you would it, you rude arsehole, she muttered to herself. She took their hot drinks into them just as Ray was removing his latest box of luxury chocolate biscuits from his bottom drawer, then she watched Finn select one of the two she'd licked the day before and she smiled a secret smile; she really must think of a new punishment for the rudeness, she needed the boost.

Ray and Finn spent the next hour discussing business details until, at nine thirty, Sophie informed them that the first patient had arrived, Miss Charlotte Stephens. Ray stood up as two young women entered his office, both quick to sit down once invited. Ray noticed that both were of average height and weight if somewhat shabbily dressed and he could not deny the word 'common' floating through his thoughts. Finn sat away from the scene, discretely in one corner, out of their direct line of vision.

"So, which one of you is Charlotte?" asked Ray, noticing the poorly dyed hair and lip piercings on both girls.

"I am," said a heavily made-up, short haired girl with large, gold hoop earrings. "This is my sister Olivia. She told me I should come and see you because she came here two years ago and she said you looked after her."

"OK Charlotte, can I ask how old you are?"

"I'm eighteen,"

"And how far along are you?"

"Don't know exactly, a few months I suppose."

"So, you're not exactly sure when your last period was?"

"No, not really, I don't track it that closely."

"Do you have a regular partner?"

"I did, but we split up last week. He doesn't know I'm up the duff and I'm not going to tell him. I just want it sorted."

"Right, I'll need to examine you and do an ultra-sound test, to get a rough idea of how far advanced your pregnancy is and I'll need to take a blood sample. Do you have any medical conditions, take any medication, is your general health good?"

"I'm fine and not taking any medicines."

"Do you smoke, drink alcohol, use recreational drugs or anything I should know about?"

"I like some wine and ciggies, but I don't do drugs at all." Twenty minutes later after a brief examination and a scan, Charlotte was deemed to be in good health and approximately three months pregnant.

"OK Charlotte, all seems to be fine. If you see my secretary before you leave and make an appointment for a Thursday. You'll need to avoid all alcohol for at least three days before you return and we'll need payment on arrival. Sophie will give you the details. Goodbye for now." As Ray stood up and walked to open the door it was quite clear that the appointment was over, so Charlotte and Olivia left without saying another word. Finn nodded at Ray, obviously impressed with the detached yet efficient professionalism of his partner.

"Good candidate, as long as the blood comes back clean, but you're possibly being too particular. Now we need plenty more where she came from, eh?"

"You're right Finn, we need to increase the merchandise; too many girls taking the NHS route."

"Well I have a few ideas on that line, which we can discuss after dinner tonight. How many more appointments do you have today?"

"Six I think, but not all stay with us when they know a quick fix costs them £300."

#

Dinner that evening was less than relaxing for Beth, painfully aware as she was of Finn's gaze on her throughout most of the meal. He questioned her about school and friends, in his mind trying to include her in the conversation, but to Beth it felt more like an interrogation. He had bought an expensive bottle of red wine to have with the meal and, as was usual, Beth was allowed a small glass when they had company. As Molly carried dinner plates out to the kitchen and Ray left to answer the telephone in the hall, Beth excused herself briefly to avoid being left alone with Finn. She headed for the bathroom, listening carefully for a couple of minutes for her parents return to the dining room before she returned herself. Finn took the opportunity, alone in the room, to pop a familiar small olive-green tablet into Beth's glass, then watched it quickly dissolve. He'd enjoy the results of his little green friend later, he thought, smiling secretly to himself as Ray sat down.

Molly was soon back, carrying a deliciously extravagant looking dessert in her hands, both men watching expectantly as she served them a generous portion each. Beth returned too but was quite sure she could not stomach such a rich pudding without vomiting in front of everyone, so she declined politely. Ten minutes later she stood to leave the table, not having tasted even a sip of her wine.

"Beth, please sit and enjoy this beautiful wine I've brought from Switzerland, it's one of our finest," Finn prompted.

"Thank you but I have loads of homework tonight and I need to concentrate. Please excuse me." She was gone and both Ray and Molly knew they would not see her again that evening.

"No point in wasting it," said Molly as she reached for the glass; Finn sat and watched her empty the glass in four successive swigs, aware that, for now, his plans had been thwarted.

"Well that was a scrumptious meal Molly, thank you, but Ray and I must now retreat and get back to business, if you'll excuse us."

"Right, fine," put in Ray, confused by his partner's slightly gruff statement, "let's go then." Molly remained seated at the table and noticed there was still at least half a glass of wine left in the bottle, so she reached for it and emptied it into the glass she'd inherited from Beth. 'I've earned this today,' she thought to herself, as she sipped and savoured the last few swallows of red nectar contentedly.

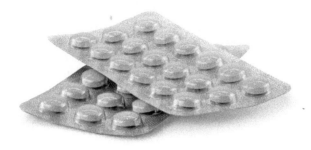

#

Across town, Kate and Wilf were also enjoying a post-dinner glass of quality red wine, snuggled up together on their huge, squashy sofa in front of a crackling log fire. They sat in luxurious silence for a while, both watching golden flames play hide and seek, flashing at them momentarily before instantly ducking behind the logs again. Wilf broke the silence with his gentle, chocolate brown voice.

"You've been very pensive all week Kate; is something worrying you that I should know about? You're not ill, are you?"

Kate knew that, in the warmth and comfort of Wilf's arms, she could unload her thoughts, confident that he was absolutely reliable regarding the confidentiality required of her job.

"No, no, I'm fit as a fiddle, you know I am. It's just that I have a patient who so reminds me of myself as a teenager and I can't explain why, but I feel hugely involved, more than usual and more than I should. She's in the same predicament I was in at seventeen, but she's underage and adamant she's still a virgin….. and, for the first time in a long time, I don't know how to handle the situation."

"Well it's not really your problem, is it love? You must be guided by the medical rules that you've always followed in the past, give her and her parents all the options available and let them take responsibility for the decision on outcome." Wilf was always ready to listen and then give a sensible response.

"The trouble is Wilf, that the girl in question refuses to confide in her parents, she's something of a loner and in classic denial, maintaining she's as innocent sexually as the day is long. She's a nice girl Wilf and I instinctively want to believe her, but the pregnancy test proved positive and she won't let me help her."

"You can't do anything to help her if she won't let you love, you just have to let it go until she asks for help. If she can't talk to her parents, she'll doubtless come to you in due course, when she's either ready or desperate."

"But what if she's being abused Wilf? What if she's being forced by someone and yet, psychologically, she's separated herself from the experience because she's too traumatised to face it?"

"Well, being just a humble builder, my medical knowledge is bordering on zero, but you've told me before that psychology and counselling are not your area of expertise as a GP, are they love? If you think she's in danger you have to call Child Protection, don't you?"

"I don't know. The parents are social climbers, selfish, arrogant, more concerned with status than their daughter, but I've known them for years and I don't believe they're the types to abuse her, even though most abuse goes on in the home, as we all know. No, they're both too concerned with other people's opinions of them to risk any sort of scandal."

"I'm going to pour us both another glass of this lovely wine. You relax, try to put this whole thing out of your mind and, I'm sure, something will happen which will make it clear to you what you should do. Until then you can do nothing." With that, he kissed her on the top of her head and disappeared into the kitchen.

#

Molly was not feeling too well as she tried to rinse the dishes off under the hot water prior to stacking them in the dishwasher. Her head began to swim and she had to give into the overwhelming need to lie down; uncharacteristically, she turned and walked away from the detritus in her kitchen and headed towards the stairs, clutching on to the banisters to haul herself upwards and into her bedroom, where she collapsed on to the bed moments before passing out completely, her last thought being that she really had drunk too much wine.

#

Beth tapped away at numbers on her mobile and sat on her bed, waiting for Joe to pick up.

"Hey, what are you up to? Are you babysitting Freddy tonight?"

"No, the three of us are playing cards, what are you doing?

"Homework. I'm desperate. Anything is better than sitting at the table with dad's nauseating partner."

"Whoa, that's no way to talk about your mum Beth!"

"Silly, you know who I mean. You're so lucky Joe. Dad and sleaze-bag Finn are in the study and mum's drunk on her bed. Why do parents get drunk? It's disgusting. I hate it."

"Poor you. Want to come over? I'm sure mum would run you home later."

"No, it's too late and I have my first exam next week, so I should study really. The next few weeks are going to be hell, I can't wait for the exams to be over."

"OK, well if you're sure. Cheer up, we'll be forty before we know it and the exams will just be a distant memory. See you at the bus stop in the morning. G'night." Joe went back to his card game as Beth clicked off her phone and sat quietly for a few moments, before rolling up her T-shirt and observing her stomach and her breasts.

Why did her period only last a couple of days and why were her boobs so large and tender? She couldn't come up with an answer. Perhaps she should return to Kate Monroe and let her do another blood test after all, because her hormones were *definitely* not quite right, but she remembered her last anxious conversation with Kate and quickly put the idea of returning to one side. No, the best thing to do was to pull down her shirt again, stop worrying, ignore everything, concentrate on her exams and let her body sort itself out. In roughly four to six weeks time her next period would be normal, when the stress of exams was behind her and she could relax again. Nothing to care about after that except how to enjoy seven weeks of school holidays. With new resolve, she reached over the side of her bed for her bag and pulled out her copy of Romeo and Juliet, then switched on her laptop and immersed herself in her revision.

#

Martha looked up as Joe returned to the table to resume their game of whist.

"Who was on the phone, was it Beth again?" she asked.

"Yes, it was. She has the worst parents mum; they don't give a stuff about her truly and I think she's miserable at the moment. She's just not the Beth I know, for some reason, but she says nothing's wrong."

"Well you can't force her to share her worries. You're right, she hasn't been blessed with the most considerate parents Joe, but you shouldn't judge them because you never know what's going on in people's private lives. I'll admit though, Beth did seem uncommunicative and withdrawn when I drove her home the other night. Now come on, it's your deal." Joe shared out the cards as he spoke.

"I've been going into that house regularly for five years now mum and there's something missing. There's no warmth, no caring, just concern over appearances. Why don't Beth's parents love her the way you love us mum?"

"All people are different Joe and I'm sure they love Beth in their own way. Now focus on the game, or we won't finish it before Freddy's bedtime."

#

In the study, Finn sat in the large, comfy leather armchair as Ray handed him a glass of whisky.

"So, what are your ideas for increasing 'merchandise' Finn, are you going to let me in on them?"

"Yes Ray, but you have to be open minded about the main one."

"OK, fire away," and he sat down with his own glass, wondering what radical ideas this man could come up with that he, Ray, had failed to do.

"Right, bare facts. We need to be more productive if this liaison with your company, S.K.I.L.L., is going to work and earn us both some money. We need more quality, reliable 'goods' to work with and we need them on a relatively regular basis. We have investment sorted, huge investment from various sources, as we discussed previously, so now we need to make plans on how best to use that investment. Tell me Ray, what group of people in our community is generally strong and disease free, lacking in too many moral hang-ups but willing to fight for people's rights, plus most in need of cash?" Finn gazed at Ray with a smug smile on his face, waiting for an answer.

"Well, kids I suppose," Ray answered confused, not sure where this conversation was going.

"Not kids Ray, students, preferably overseas students with less than a perfect command of the English language. Full of life and enthusiasm, free of parental constrictions for the first time, ready to take life by the throat and get on with it. Ready to get involved in projects that help them avoid life-long debt Ray. Yes, students are the way forward, I'm sure of it."

"I'm not quite sure if we're on the same page Finn, explain exactly what you mean."

"Well think about it. What student wouldn't take the opportunity to earn up to £6,000 a year tax free, to fend off debt and provide some flexible cash?"

"Yes, but how, I'm not sure I understand."

"We butter them up with a talk or presentation on our research into life threatening illness and how our work could improve the life quality and longevity of folks worldwide. Then we offer an opportunity for them to get involved, with little or no inconvenience to them personally bar a few visits to us each year."

"Right, tell me more. How do they earn £6,000 then?"

"We run a student sponsorship programme, on the face of it to support education; at the end of each academic term, we transfer £2,000 each into their banks and in return they get pregnant Ray, two to three times per year. Each time they come in for an abortion at about eight weeks gestation, we sort them out and register them for a £2,000 sponsorship donation for the following term; as you know, it's not ethical to pay for such 'co-operation' strictly speaking and we need to stay legal. We keep the 'goods,' they go off and get pregnant again a couple of months later or as often as they need cash. Simple. What do you think?"

Ray was thoughtful for a moment.

"I don't know. Sounds feasible in theory, but how do we know they're disease free, that their 'partners' aren't riddled with chlamydia or whatever?"

"Simple blood tests Ray. Also, if we register both partners and they become regular contributors, it will be a condition of their continued participation. Full-proof. Brilliant. You must admit it's a great idea?"

"What about the legal aspects Finn? We need to remain approved by the Regional Deanery Ethical Committee to stay in practice. Also, how vulnerable would we be to litigation if someone suffered complications?"

"Firstly, thirty per cent of our practice will be above board, to keep the R.D.E.C. happy and off our backs, whilst seventy per cent of it will be under their radar and they'll be blissfully unaware of it. As for the students Ray, they are adults. They sign an agreement confirming that they joined the research of their own free will, no pressure, aware of the very minimal risks involved."

"OK, but we both know that there can be considerable physical risks on occasion, not to mention emotional side effects. We don't want to be sued out of existence."

"I repeat Ray, they sign a waiver at the start, confirming that they chose to join the sponsorship research and wanted to take a small part in medical advancement." For the next few hours, the two of them discussed possible pitfalls, legalities, insurance, recruitment, the whole package, Ray playing devil's advocate at every turn. Finn had an answer for every challenge though, becoming more impatient with every query and eventually playing his winning card.

"Look Ray, are you in or out, because our sponsors will walk away from S.K.I.L.L. unless you start playing the bigger game and they won't wait for much longer."

"OK Finn, let's put this into action, I'm convinced. Next step is to plan recruitment, adverts for students, work out a presentation which can be delivered in the conference room at S.K.I.L.L., plus a contract of sorts. It's May now and we need to be up and running in time for the next influx of students in September, so let's get down to business."

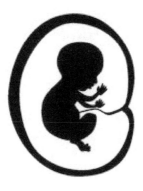

#

The next month was a whirl of activity for Beth and she seemed to lose all sense of time, swamped by study leave and revision and one exam after another. She missed seeing Joe each morning, but she enjoyed meeting up after each exam and going over it question by question. They were both so relieved when the final paper was done and they could just chill out for the rest of the summer. On the final Friday afternoon, having walked away from school hand in hand, they lay flat on their backs on the grass in the park, enjoying the warm sun on their faces, watching the fluffy clouds drift lazily across the clear, blue sky.

"Thank goodness we're free of books, of study leave, of exams, of teachers, of the whole bloody lot of it ...... for now; let's really make the most of this summer Joe."

"Yes and you can relax and return to being the real Beth," replied Joe without thinking.

"What do you mean, '*the real Beth*,' Joe?"

"Just that you've been different over the last few months, not yourself. Not really surprising when you consider the pressure we've been living with because of exams, plus your home life isn't as laid back as mine. Your dad brings tension home because of his busy work life and mine is rarely home at all. Your mum is neurotic and mine is so easy going she's almost horizontal. This means we live in very different atmospheres each and every day, so it's bound to rub off on us both and I can't imagine how you've survived the last couple of months without peace at home."

"It's normal for me though, I've never known it any different," she replied somewhat sadly. As they both lay still, silently thinking of what Beth had just said, she was suddenly aware of the most peculiar sensation in her lower belly, like a butterfly trying to escape from a bubble. Beth leapt to her feet and grabbed her bag in a frenzied instant. "I have to go. I need the loo urgently," and just like that she was gone. She sprinted away across the grass and down to the pavement, as Joe's gaze followed her until she had turned a corner. 'Have I upset her or said the wrong thing?' he pondered, as he sat staring into the space that had moments ago been occupied by Beth.

#

Molly was sitting at her kitchen table with a hot cuppa when she heard Beth dash in through the front door and positively thunder up the staircase, despite the skinny trainers she always wore these days. This was followed by the bathroom door slamming shut, then silence.

Beth sat on the toilet, waiting for the arrival of the upset tummy she had been expecting, but nothing happened. As she sat there, not sure whether to stay or leave, it happened again, that unmistakeable trapped butterfly feeling. 'What *is* that,' she wondered; 'I haven't eaten anything unusual or spicy or over-fruity, and I'm still not pooing,' she realised after five minutes of waiting. Then the thought hit her like a runaway train – no period for three months, apart from those two days after she'd last seen Kate Monroe. In something of a daze, she returned to her bedroom and stood in front of her mirror, trying to pluck up the courage to raise her T-shirt and look at her sideways profile. Just as she did this her heart froze, as she noticed the reflection of her mother standing in the doorway.

"You're getting fat Beth, I've thought so once or twice lately. Have you been eating junk food whilst you've been out with Joe, because you haven't eaten much in the way of home dinners recently?" Beth struggled to hide the fear in her voice.

"Yeah, may-be," she stammered; "It's hard when you come out of an exam, you're suddenly starving, so you head for the comfort food I suppose."

"Well you need to be more careful now that the exams are over. I don't want people thinking I've got a fat daughter who hasn't been taught better. I'll prepare a salad for you tonight, no more stodgy pies at Joe's house for a while. I'll give you some money for bigger clothes tomorrow and you can go shopping – nothing like tight clothes to emphasise bulk," then she went back downstairs to her cooling cuppa. Beth sat on her bed, reached down to the floor for her laptop and typed in 'early signs of pregnancy,' then sat and waited for the screen to tell her a pack of lies.

#

Sophie had been looking at the holiday offers in her magazine when Ray and Finn marched from the main office into the reception area. She quickly shoved the magazine under her desk, grabbed the phone and began talking to an imaginary caller.

"Yes, that's fine, all booked in for you for next week. Bye now," then she looked up and smiled as the two men arrived at her desk.

"We're leaving now and we won't be back until the morning Sophie. There are some important recordings on my dictaphone which I want typed up before you leave tonight – have them on my desk first thing in the morning. We'll be in early to go through them, so don't forget," Ray instructed without even looking at her, then strode out with his usual air of arrogant confidence.

"Shit, shit and shit again," Sophie said aloud to an empty room. She had hoped to leave early tonight as she had an 'eyebrows and armpits' appointment at the beauticians at 6.30pm and she wanted to dash home for a shower first, but those plans were now spoiled. So, a spot of social justice was required to pick up her spirits nicely, prior to starting work on those documents. She sat thinking for a moment, then her petite body rose from her desk like a diva on a West End stage, all elegance and poise. Her slim hips hugged by her red pencil skirt, long sleek auburn hair flowing over her shoulders, toned legs perfectly balanced on her customary six-inch-high heels, her movements were totally wasted on an empty room yet satisfyingly ego-boosting.

Once in Ray's office, having opened his bottom drawer gently, Sophie lifted out his prize chocolate biscuits again and was about to remove the lid when she noticed something altogether more tempting further back in the drawer. It was a small, white box with gold writing on it – 'Chanel No 5.' Sophie's heart raced a little faster as her new plan of revenge took shape in her risky imagination. She returned to her own desk and, in the bottom drawer, delved into her handbag for the tiniest, finest pair of nail scissors.

Back in the main office with her reward in her hand, she turned the box of perfume upside down and began very carefully to tease the cellophane fold apart, taking great care not to tear it. Little by little the clear, thin plastic was eased free of itself, exposing the bottom fold of the box and, once again, the delicate scissors performed brilliantly in unfolding the flap of card. That done, the bottle dropped out of the box neatly into Sophie's eagerly awaiting hand; within moments, the glorious aroma of expensive perfume was on her neck, wrists and thighs (a must, as warm air rises, we all know that).

Like an experienced thief Sophie set about returning everything to its original, unsuspicious state, finishing with the finest dab of transparent nail polish from her handbag to fix the cellophane shut, then replacing the reassembled package at the back of the drawer. As a final touch of revenge therapy, she repeated her normal trick of expertly running her tongue along two of the biscuits, then returning them in the box to the drawer.

'Now, to work,' she smiled, as she wafted in a haze of Chanel to her own desk with dictaphone in hand, puzzling over the fact that a rude, unpleasant man like Ray would ever think to buy perfume at all. 'Must be on a promise from old prickly pants Molly,' she thought as she booted up her computer screen.

#

JUNE

Kate Monroe finished signing referral letters, switched off her computer and tidied her desk and was on the point of closing her diary when Beth Gregson suddenly popped into her mind. She flicked back through the pages of her diary to where she had written, in bold letters, 'NB: Pt 2601? HCG' two months earlier. 'Mmmmm, still no contact from Beth Gregson and she is into her second trimester by now, unless she miscarried without realising it. Poor girl, what must she be going through and how on earth can I help her when she rejects every effort I make?' Kate pondered for a while and resolved to take action the following day, but she'd have to decide on what form that would take tonight, at home, with Wilf's help.

#

Martha shut the front door gently behind her and slipped off her shoes, then tip-toed silently down the dimly lit hall and into the homely sitting room. Joe's long legs were curled under him on the sofa, as he quietly strummed his guitar by the soft light of a single lamp on the coffee table.

"Hi mum, where have you been tonight? There's a hot cuppa in the pot on the table if you want one. Freddy's been asleep since 8pm, a bit off-colour, just a cold I think," Joe reported amiably.

"Thanks love, didn't you find my note telling you about dinner and my meeting?"

"Yes, but you didn't say where or what meeting it was."

"Oh, it was SPUC again and we've decided to hold monthly silent prayer vigils outside the hospital on abortion days. We can't do every abortion day, which is Wednesday and Saturday afternoons, but once a month is a start at least."

"What do you hope to achieve, if it's silent prayer?" Joe waited for an answer as he watched his mum slump exhaustedly on to the sofa and curl her legs up under her mirroring him, then sigh with relief.

"Well, firstly you mustn't underestimate the power of prayer Joe, especially when there are a number of people present each time. Those poor, lost little souls need our prayers, as do their parents. Secondly, we'll silently hold up posters which will include messages of support for pregnant women who might want an alternative to abortion and not know how to access it; also, for post-abortion sufferers, who might need support or counselling. Just pictures, messages and prayer; no judgement, just support."

"Wow, that's a big step. Aren't you worried about anger, abuse or even attack from unsympathetic people? Do you need a police presence?"

"No Joe, that's why it will be silent prayer. It tends to be vocal protests that incite anger and those poor victims inside the hospital are suffering far more, aren't they? Now, stop worrying and pour me a cuppa, there's a love." Joe reached for the teapot, but it didn't stop him thinking about his mum's words and worrying for her safety. He occasionally felt the weight of a responsibility that should have been on his dad's shoulders instead of his, but he didn't resent it; he'd just have to keep an eye on his mum, he could see that.

#

Kate lay back in a hot, scented bath, luxuriating in the velvety smooth bubbles surrounding her and the sweet smell of jasmine, which was wafting up from the ten little candles sitting comfortingly around the edge of the bathtub. Wilf walked into the steamy haven and handed her a glass of chilled Chablis, her favourite, as he sat down on the velour topped linen basket beside the bath. His slightly-too-long brown hair soon absorbed the damp and flopped lazily down on to his forehead as he gazed at her intently, trying to read the deep, faraway expression in her eyes as she lay there, lost in thought.

"Glad your working week is over? Relax, enjoy, sip your wine, more where that came from with dinner. Happy?"

"Supremely, I'm so lucky to have you. What's for dinner?"

"Surprise, but you'll like it." The cool wine slipping down through her body created a noticeable contrast to her hot skin, but she loved the dual sensations. She paused for a few moments before she spoke again.

"I've made a decision Wilf, about my life, about our lives." Wilf wanted Kate to relax, it was Friday evening and she lived such a pressurised life as a GP; but he knew her well enough that when she wanted to speak there was no stopping her, whether the subject was major or minor.

"Tell me," was his calm response.

"Over the last month, largely due to this patient I told you about, I've come to accept that life has no predictable rhyme or reason, it just is. We have to accept our lot, make peace with it and be excessively grateful for the good things that happen, not grieve excessively for the things we can't change." She paused, thinking privately for a few moments.

"Where is this going Kate? Are you sure you're not ill?"

"No love, I'd tell you if I were, but I think I've been grieving for far too long over the fact that we can't have children, instead of accepting it and moving on. It's not meant to be. Simple."

"OK, so what's the decision? We already discussed and rejected the ideas of fostering or adoption, it's not for us."

"No, nothing so life changing. It's just that I'm ready to clear the nursery, get rid of the clothes and the bits of furniture, let it go and stop grieving. I've tortured myself and you for long enough, I have to forgive myself and just enjoy what we have together."

"You are blameless Kate, I've never held you responsible, we did our best."

"I know, I know, but I blamed me, in my heart. I have to forgive myself for me, not you. So, let's clear the room this weekend, give everything to charity or something and turn the room into a hobby room; let's take up a new hobby together, golf may-be, guitar, or even archery and we'll use the room to store golf clubs, arrows, whatever. I'm ready, are you?" Wilf smiled, leaned over to kiss her gently, then clinked their glasses together and took a huge swig, downing the rest of his wine in one go.

"Give me your glass, I'll go and top us up," he said as he left the room grinning happily.

#

JULY

Beth and Joe laughed and squealed with the ecstasy of perceived freedom, as they romped in his garden hitting an old badminton shuttlecock over a piece of unravelling rope, tied between the fence and apple tree. It was bliss to be in shorts and t-shirts on a weekday instead of their tiresome school uniform and they chased around like a couple of five-year-olds in the bright afternoon sun. Martha watched them from the kitchen window for a few minutes, noticing that Beth wasn't quite the skinny girl she had been; not that she was fat, just somewhat thicker around the middle.

After another long rally, the pair of them collapsed on to the grass, giggling hysterically, struggling to catch their breath. Martha decided to take them some cold squash to quench their thirst and, a few minutes later, she sat down on the grass beside them with a tray, a jug of orange and three glasses.

"You two are having fun. It's clear that exams are now an unwelcome memory and it's so nice to hear you laughing again. Here, have a drink." Beth emptied her glass in three long gulps, then lay back on the grass and shut her eyes. As Martha studied her and smiled down at this sweet girl, she suddenly became aware of the unmistakable bump under Beth's t-shirt, a clearly pregnant tummy which had been very flat just a couple of months ago. The realisation of the implications hit her like a thundering train out of control.

"Oh, my word," she screeched before she could stop herself.

"What mum, what is it?" Joe was immediately concerned at her distress, whilst Beth sat bolt upright and met Martha's gaze head-on.

The shock of their mutual knowledge prevented Martha from speaking, then she mumbled something about a pan of potatoes on the stove and disappeared rapidly into the house.

"That was strange, she doesn't normally cook potatoes at two in the afternoon or forget about them. I hope she's ok," Joe commented with a vague air of concern. "Come on, let's carry on our game."

"No, I should go, mum's taking me shopping in a while. Say 'bye and thanks' to your mum for me," and Joe was all alone in a flash.

#

Beth didn't go home to go shopping with her mum; instead she went to the surgery and asked to see Kate Monroe. She stood anxiously in front of the glass screen over the clinical white counter, waiting for a positive reaction as the receptionist rose from her desk and walked towards her.

"I'm sorry, but Dr. Monroe is on holiday for four weeks. Would you like an appointment with another doctor?", the receptionist asked kindly.

"No, NO, it must be Dr Monroe, when will she be back?" Beth's response sounded forceful, even to herself. She tried to calm her nerves. "Sorry, but Dr Monroe asked me to call back any time I needed, so it must be her."

"OK, she'll be back on Monday the 28th August, shall I book you in for 9am?"

"Yes, thank you," and Beth left the surgery, wondering whether Martha would tell Joe what she was now certain was no longer just her secret fear.

#

The following week, Joe and Beth found themselves amongst a highly excited crowd in the school corridor, hardly able to hear themselves think for the exalted level of decibels in the confined space. Dozens of students anxiously awaited the results of their exams to be handed out to them, tension mounting with every passing second. Moments later, the overwhelming sound was of tearing paper, as envelopes were ripped open frantically. Typically, Joe and Beth extricated themselves from the throng and left quickly, heading back to their favourite patch of grass in the park before daring to open their envelopes. Staring each other in the eyes, Beth said quietly:

"After three …… one, two, three." Both stared at their results sheets, absorbing the information intently, before locking eyes again; gradually a smile spread across both of their faces and Joe whooped for joy.

"Six A's and four B's, how about you?"

"Two A's, seven B's and a C, so not bad. Yay," as her hands flew up into the air.

"Phew, what a relief, my mum will be thrilled. What shall we do to celebrate?" Beth was less ecstatic, thinking of the response she'd get at her home.

"I'm not sure my parents have even remembered it's results day, but they'll be relieved just the same when I tell them. Let's go and get an ice-cream for starters and then a burger, I'm starving."

#

Martha was in a quandary, worried sick about the implications of Beth's pregnancy on Joe; he was too young to be a father at sixteen years old, too young to sacrifice his freedom to a life of responsibility, too young to walk away from education. She thought she knew her son, they were normally so open with each other, so why would he not tell her of their predicament? Did he even know about Beth's condition? As for Beth - she knew Beth to be a sweet girl, unlucky enough to have awful parents, a girl who had few real friends; she could not believe Beth would spend so much time with Joe if she had another boyfriend, so Joe must be the father. What to do, what to say, should she wait for Joe to speak or bring up the subject herself? It was at times like this that she wished Jack was not away so much, that she wished she could discuss the boys with him in person, not on the phone; should she even worry him with this before she was sure?

#

AUGUST

Arriving at her surgery early on 28th August, Kate looked at her appointments schedule for the day and noticed Beth Gregson was her first patient. Thankful that she was relaxed after her month away, Kate wondered whether she would be presented with a noticeably more pregnant Beth, or whether there had actually been a miscarriage during the early bleed; either way, she would need to examine Beth thoroughly and also address the issue of possible abuse of an underage child. As Beth walked in a short while later, Kate recognised instantly that there had been no miscarriage. She smiled widely.

"Beth, how lovely to see you, how are things?"

"Well, as you can may-be work out, you were right all along. I'm sorry if I was rude, but I really didn't believe I was pregnant and I still don't know how it happened. I haven't ever had sex, truly, so how can this be happening to me? What should I do?" Instantly the tears were flowing, great gulps of distress issuing from Beth's throat, great globs of snot pouring from her nose. "I don't know what to do, what should I do?" Kate passed her a handful of tissues and fetched her a glass of water from the basin in the corner, feeling concerned but relieved that Beth was, finally, facing the truth. Kate's tone was gentle but assured.

"Right, sip your water and let's try to work out exactly how far along you are, then we'll discuss your options, ok?" Beth mopped her face whilst Kate opened her diary. "Now, looking at my calendar and remembering that your first two periods were somewhat erratic, you must be somewhere between fifteen and twenty weeks gone. Also, bearing in mind how young you are, you need to decide whether you want to proceed with the pregnancy, which will involve including your parents in this, or whether you want to think about a termination. It's become a fairly urgent decision now, so is there anyone you can confide in, to help you make up your mind?" Calmer now, but very miserable faced with the truth, Beth looked forlorn.

"I don't know, may-be, but not my parents, not yet."

"Alright, hop up on to the bed and I'll take a look at you, feel your tummy and listen for the baby's heartbeat, check your blood pressure and so on, then we'll talk some more." Kate's kind, confident calmness was reassuring to Beth and she felt herself begin to trust that Kate would help her. A short while later, Beth sat up and pulled her large T-shirt back down over her belly.

"Well, all seems to be ok, you're a young, healthy person Beth, but we need to arrange a scan to be sure all is well and to help us work out more accurately how far along you are. I'll phone the gynaecology consultant at the hospital to see if there are any free slots this week, the sooner the better. Now hop down and sit on the chair, we need to talk about one more thing." Beth sat on the chair, again feeling trapped but somehow more accepting of the situation. "You're fifteen Beth, underage, so I'm concerned for your safety and how you came to be pregnant. By rights, I should have referred you to a social worker when you first came to see me, for your own protection."

"No, I'm sixteen, I had my birthday a few weeks ago, so you don't need to worry about that now."

"But are you sure no-one's forcing you to do things you're not happy with? Is anyone putting pressure on you, are you scared of anyone? You were still underage when this happened Beth."

"No, I don't remember anything happening, no-one's forcing me to do anything. Home is normal, mum and dad are ok, no-one ever comes to stay except dad's horrid partner Finn, so it's ok." Thinking back and suddenly aware of deeply embedded memories, Kate forced herself to ask:

"Did you go to any parties around March / April time, where something might have happened?" Beth shook her head but said nothing.

Kate pondered for a moment, then spoke. "So, Beth, you don't have sex with your boyfriend and the only person who ever stays at your house is your father's partner, have I understood that correctly?" Beth nodded, but she could see the question on Kate's face and spoke before it could be asked.

"I'm not sleeping with dad's partner, if that's what you're thinking. Yew, the very thought's disgusting, he's old, he's at least forty-five, yuk," and the expression on her face spoke a thousand words.

"OK, we'll leave that for now, if you're certain you don't feel in any danger. Now, before you leave, I'll call the gynaecologist and see if I can get you in for a quick scan appointment," and Beth looked on as Kate picked up the phone.

#

It was Monday morning and Sophie was in the conference suite, busily setting out chairs and tables for the first incoming group of students. The room was large and bright with huge windows all along one wall, expensively accompanied by vertical blinds, the new air conditioning making it comfortably cool compared to the temperature outside. She placed a bottle of water and paper cups in the centre of each table, plus a pile of carefully worded provisional contracts and half a dozen pens. Today was the first presentation of the student recruitment scheme, with twenty-four students expected at 3pm. Ray was to present the medical aspects and the huge contribution the students would be making to stem cell research, with their possible involvement in finding cures for a multitude of degenerative diseases, a heavy dose of social conscience included. Finn was to explain the very tempting financial gains to be had by taking part in the research – emphasis on sponsorship, NOT payment -what student wouldn't be tempted by a relatively easily accessible £6,000 each year? The possible risks to student health and well-being and future fertility would be touched on very lightly, as would the mandatory disclaimer to be signed on the contract. All legal bases were covered as far as Ray and Finn were concerned and if any participants were to suffer side effects, well, there were plenty more students where they came from.

Sophie was happy with her job. She didn't like the rude way Ray spoke to her on a daily basis and she didn't particularly like the practices that went on at S.K.I.L.L., but as long as she didn't think about it too much she was alright. Apart from Ray she was answerable to no-one and she enjoyed her healthy wages at the end of each month, so the world was hunky-dory as far as she was concerned. She finally checked that the computer was set up and ready for the power point presentation, then she left the room, quietly shutting the door behind her.

#

As Beth lay on the hard bed in a bright and very clinical room, feeling extremely exposed and vulnerable all on her own, heart racing twenty to the dozen, she watched nervously as the nurse spread clear, cold jelly all over her swollen belly. Then an instrument like a microphone, which must have been a camera of sorts, was pressed against her flesh, sliding backwards and forwards through the jelly as it sent images of something dark and mysterious on to a small screen beside the bed. The nurse concentrated on the screen without saying a word for a couple of minutes, then turned to Beth and smiled kindly.

"All seems to be normal, nothing obvious to worry about, would you like to see your baby?"

"No, what, I don't know. How can you tell that grey mess is a baby?" she stammered.

"Look here," the nurse said turning the screen towards Beth, "this is the baby's head, here are the legs and those dots are the baby's spine; this black, flickering blob is the baby's heart beating, about 120 times per minute, see?" Beth was mesmerised as she slowly made sense of the darkness on the screen, shocked into silence. "I can't tell you what sex the baby is because of the way it's lying, but may-be next time you come we'll have a clearer view. I'll print off a picture for you to keep."

"No!" came a quick response which, even to Beth, sounded shockingly aggressive. "No, thank you," more calmly this time, as she watched the jelly being wiped away with generous handfuls of tissue.

"Right, no problem, I'll send the results through to your GP and you'll need to see her for monthly check-ups for a while, OK?" A silent nod was the only response. Within ten minutes, Beth was again sitting on the top, quiet deck of a bus home, trying to mentally digest what she had just experienced.

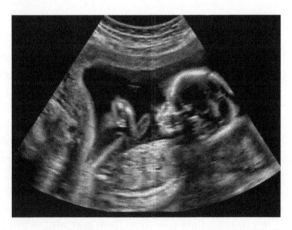

#

Martha's concern for her son was too overwhelming to be ignored, so she resolved to broach her fears over Beth with him that evening, once Freddy was asleep. She had to somehow give Joe an opening to confide in her if he needed to, because this was too much responsibility for a boy of sixteen to handle alone, wasn't it? Or was she just serving her own curiosity? She was so terrified for her son that she couldn't analyse her own feelings, all objectivity was gone. Sitting on the sofa some hours later, lost in her own panic, she was suddenly brought back to the present when Joe spoke loudly to her.

"Mum, I've asked you twice what is on your mind, you're so distant and preoccupied tonight."

"Sorry love, just lost in my own thoughts, that's all."

"I know you better than that mum, what is it? Is there a problem with Freddy, is he in trouble at school? He's a lazy little turd but he's not in any bother that he's told me about, I'd tell you straight away."

"No, it's nothing, just tired, ignore me. Cuppa?" She was in the kitchen in a flash and Joe listened to the familiar sound of mugs being filled and biscuits being plonked on to a plate.

"How's Beth?" she asked as she placed the tray on the small table in between them.

"Fine, I saw her this afternoon, why?"

"No reason, I just wondered how you were both doing, if your relationship was changing, stuff like that."

"Where's this coming from mum? She's my closest friend and I'm hers, end of. My feelings for her are changing a bit, to be honest, we're not ten any more, but not sure about hers."

"Does she have other friends, a boyfriend, or does she rely on you?"

"'Course she has other friends, one or two anyway, but I'm her closest; she's private like me, not gregarious; we understand each other completely, but she has been more distant lately for some reason. Her parents are weird, it's not an easy home life, I don't know how she copes with it to be honest." Molly sipped her tea and nibbled on a biscuit, waiting for him to say more, but he didn't.

#

For a few weeks the weather had been unbearably hot and humid because of the uncharacteristic heatwave enveloping the country, with temperatures of 30-35 degrees Celsius constantly reported on the television. A nationwide hose-pipe ban had been enforced and there were sporadic outbursts of moorland fires up and down the country, keeping firefighters busy around the clock.

Beth found the heat difficult to take, particularly at night when her bedroom was so stuffy and humid; her mother had told her to leave her window and door open to allow a through draft, so she began sleeping on top of her bed to stay cool, keeping just a sheet over her to hide her growing bump, in case her mother walked in whilst she was asleep - not that she'd made a habit of that for a few years. Still, no point in taking any risks.

Lazing on the grass in Joe's garden or at the park had been abandoned, the ground was so hard and dry and uncomfortable. With little or no energy for anything dynamic in the heat, Joe and Beth were searching for things to do to fill the long, hot days of their precious school break.

"I know," Joe said one afternoon when they were wondering what to do, "let's go swimming in the river to cool off." This had been a regular pastime of theirs the previous two summers, so it seemed like the best idea to Joe, but Beth was too aware that her growing belly would be horribly obvious.

"No, no, can't do it sorry, um...wrong time of the month," she stuttered awkwardly.

"What? Oh, ok, so let's go and dangle our feet from the riverbank instead then, just for a while." Ten minutes later they were enjoying the cool water swishing through their toes and tickling their ankles, sitting in companionable silence on the riverbank. "Mind if I go in for a bit?" Joe asked.

"No, 'course not, go for it, I'll watch your stuff," she said as Joe peeled off his clothes down to his boxers. For the next half hour Beth watched Joe's antics in the water, floating, jumping and diving, all the while surfacing and grinning at her.

"Aren't you unbearably hot or bored?" he asked her.

"No, I'm just fine, you carry on."

"I don't believe you, you look baked," he answered, and spontaneously started splashing her with great sweeps of his hands and arms across the surface of the water.

"Stop Joe, please stop," she screamed, but it was too late, she was soaked through. Her oversized t-shirt clung to her body like cling film, simultaneously hiding and exposing her now considerable baby bump. Joe's laughter at her screams subsided as he noticed her look at her belly, realisation slowly dawning on him. Dripping with water, he walked over to her with an incredulous look on his face, shocked into near silence.

"I don't understand .... who .... when....I can't believe it," his words barely audible. After a few moments of just staring at her, anger and hurt began to seep into him. "Beth, I'm your closest friend, how could you do this without me knowing, how... how...HOW?" Beth had no words, tears welled up as she just looked him in the eyes, then she quietly stood up and walked away.

#

Back in the surgery the next day, Kate Monroe was choosing her words carefully as she sat opposite Beth, knowing that fairly urgent decisions had to be made, all the while feeling desperately sorry for this gentle girl who was facing this dilemma almost completely alone. She thought Beth looked even more desolate than before, if that were possible.

"Beth, the scan was good, the baby is healthy and you are estimated to be about twenty-two weeks into your pregnancy," Kates soft voice at odds with the words she was saying. "We now need to decide how we go forward, whether you want to keep your baby or.......not. If not, we must take fairly swift action as .....well, it's pretty urgent now. Have you spoken to your parents at all?"

"No, I can't, I just can't." An overwhelming sense of déjà vu swamped Kate as she heard her own voice, so like her mother's, stating mandatory 'common sense.'

"Beth, you're only sixteen, you're presumably starting your 'A' level studies in a couple of weeks, you have your whole life ahead of you. If you keep the baby, your parents are bound to know; if you decide not to keep it, we can sort this without them knowing, just. It will mean a termination, very soon. I'm bound to tell you though, it won't be easy, you will need support from someone following a termination, both physically and emotionally, from me but, more importantly, from someone closer to you. Is there anyone?"

"There was but now, I don't think so. Can I think about it for a couple of days please? Do I have time?"

"Yes, just, but come back to me in two days, I'll make sure I fit you in. I can only say again, if you have someone you trust, talk to them, ok? Two days, don't forget."

#

Joe sat in his bedroom, absently strumming the same chord on his guitar, over and over again, as he looked blankly at the photo on his windowsill of him and Beth in the boat.

"Joe, supper in five minutes," Martha called up the stairs to him.

"Not hungry," he called back with a discernible croak in his normally strong voice, then carried on strumming. Martha put the dinner back in the hot oven and went upstairs to Joe, knocking gently on his door as she entered and sat on his bed beside him.

"What's up Joe? Can you tell me?" He'd never been good at hiding things and Martha could see sadness and hurt etched on to his manly young face.

"It's Beth, she's been hiding something from me and I'm annoyed, no, disappointed, terribly disappointed."

"Ah, I see, can you tell me about it or not?" Joe's voice wobbled as he spoke:

"Beth's pregnant mum, pregnant, I just can't believe it. I feel so let down, but it's not as if she's my actual girlfriend is it, so why do I feel hurt?" The lack of a reaction made Joe's head shoot up suddenly and stare at his mum.

"You knew, you knew, didn't you? How did you know, why didn't you say something?"

"Well Joe, I noticed her tummy when you were in the garden playing badminton, but I was scared, shocked, I didn't know what to think. I've been scared for you Joe and what it means. I was waiting for you to speak."

"What? Why? What mum, you thought it was mine?" Joe's voice was getting higher, louder, less controlled. "No, it's not, I've done no more than hold her hand, even if I wanted to. Why would you think that?"

"I was scared Joe, I'm not aware Beth has a boyfriend other than you, you said the other day that she has few friends, what was I supposed to think?" They both sat in silence with their own thoughts for a few minutes before Molly broke that silence. "You know Joe, if she has no boyfriend, other than you I mean, then who's the father? Do you think may-be she's in danger from….someone? I know you're angry and hurt, but she may need her only real friend more than ever just now, don't you think? It's not all about you right now Joe, can you be generous enough to consider how she may be feeling? Horribly alone I imagine."

"I don't know…yes, may-be, but I need to think, leave me please." Martha gave him a hug and stood to leave, feeling his sadness as she walked out.

"I'll keep dinner warm, in case you feel hungry later. I'm just downstairs if you want to talk further."

#

Twenty new students in the S.K.I.L.L. conference room had just sat through a power-point presentation by Ray and a talk by Finn and were sitting somewhat puzzled and thoughtful when a lone voice piped up.

"What exactly does S.K.I.L.L. stand for?"

"It's an acronym for Seeking Knowledge Intent on Lengthening Life," Finn answered firmly and slowly, not sure of the boy's nationality, though he'd asked the question clearly enough. He stared confidently, almost challengingly, at the boy.

"So, let me get this right," the boy came right back at him. "You want us to each have a sex partner, the same person, throughout our student lives here, get pregnant several times a year and come here for a termination each time and, in return, you financially support our education, easing that pressure on us. But we have to stay clean, no sleeping around, no drink or drugs to excess, no freedom to explore and develop our own identities or make our own mistakes, right?"

"No way," Finn replied, a hint agitated and taken aback by the boy's level of spoken English, "you can experience all the things students so often indulge in, just not to excess, don't become addicts, stay clean. You can sleep with whoever you like, just use protection to avoid … contamination, for want of a better word – chlamydia, STD's and so on. You only have regular unprotected sex with your sex partner in this study, on two or three periods each year, to maintain your participation in this potentially life-saving research, in return for which we support your education. Straightforward, you scratch our backs and we scratch yours," Finn smiled, pleased with his handling of their first challenge to the scheme.

"Why, why are you doing this?" came the now slightly anxious response from the boy. "What if we sign up to it, then we get into a relationship and want to withdraw from it, be monogamous?"

"No problem, just respect the protection rule and don't rely on just the pill with your girlfriend … would she even have to know about your extra-relationship sex? This is stem cell research boy, the way forward into beating certain life-threatening illnesses, bringing hope to seriously ill people and their families in the long term. You'd be doing humanity a huge service; it's an opportunity to make your life really count for something and you'd benefit too, financially."

"And an opportunity to make you guys rich, right? This is big money for you, right?" The boy was now beginning to get emotional and Finn was anxious this attitude might spread around the room.

"Look, forget about the money, this is your chance to make a difference, right on the threshold of your adult life. Not many people get the chance we're offering you." Finn's tone was changing, more than a hint of annoyance creeping into his voice.

"But this is a race, right, and you want to win it, that's where the big money is, right? I'm guessing there are loads more places around the world taking part in this race too, right?" The boy was now getting louder, overtaking Finn's tone, becoming more of a threat to the status quo. Finn was beginning to lose this particular battle and he knew it, he needed to think fast, lower the tension. He took a huge breath and spoke more sympathetically, sounding far more calm than he actually felt.

"Everything's a race boy, life's one big bloody race, you just have to decide whether you want to be part of it. Just don't overthink this, you'd be donating the product of a normal human function a few times each year, ok? No big deal, you help us, we help you, simple."

"No, no. You want us make life so you can destroy, that's what I think," came the surprisingly forceful voice

71

with broken eastern-european English from a small, mousy girl on another table, so bland-looking that Finn had barely registered her presence.

"You'd be donating a clump of human cells, that's all, not lives," Finn responded rather defensively now. "At this stage of development, up to twelve weeks, the product is nothing more than a lump of human tissue, that's the point. You'd be helping to improve the quality of human life in the long term, making a valuable contribution, but there's never any gain without sacrifice is there? How many people ever get the chance we're offering you and you benefit too, no crime in that surely?"

"Clump of human cells, you say, product, are you serious?" the girl said clearly agitated, as she stood up. "These 'products' as you say, are established human lives in earliest stages, with unknown potential, skills, abilities and you want destroy them for your own gain. You could be destroying an Einstein or Darwin, next Gary Barlow or Bugsy. You don't know, do you?" She was now getting into her stride, pure force coming from such a diminutive person, leaving Finn almost speechless with surprise, but not quite.

"Look, these are human cells without thoughts, without feelings, without pain or any ability at this stage, indistinguishable from a pig foetus or a monkey foetus. No big deal ethically, but with enormous potential scientifically. Why are you even here if you feel this way? Don't let ethics stand in the way of your education, you silly girl."

"I thought you ask us donate blood, bone marrow or urine, study sleep patterns or reactions to new drugs, not hand over human embryos on regular basis. That's just murder and you want us help you. That's disgusting, immoral, horrific. Is no accident that word 'kill' is in your acronym." She was getting more emotional by the minute, potentially hysterical and Finn knew he had to calm her down.

"Look, abortion is legal up to twenty-four weeks gestation, we're / you're not breaking any laws, no need to let your conscience bother you," he replied, trying to keep his frustration with her well-hidden.

"But why the waste, why so many lives lost?" she cried.

"We can get stem cells from various sources," he countered, "from you, your bone marrow, blood and so on, but your stem cells are already programmed to do certain jobs. Foetal stem cells are more versatile, not yet programmed as such, so they have far more potential, you see, that's why. We also use umbilical stem cells for the same reason, but it's a richer crop from the foetus itself."

"Crop? Is not crop, is baby with beating heart. You're disgusting and I'm out of here. Anyone else joining me?" With that, she pushed her chair back so violently that it scraped loudly on the laminate floor jarring everyone's ears, whilst at the same time one of her arms knocked a jug of water all over the pile of provisional contracts sitting neatly in the centre of the table. "Fuck," she cried, "and fuck you," as she hurried from the room. An uncomfortable silence followed, then Finn and Ray watched as more students quietly left the room.

Sophie looked up sharply as the girl burst from the conference room, soon followed by eight more; she'd heard the commotion followed by the expletives and was not shocked to see the group leave the building.

"Good," she said out loud to herself, "that'll teach the rude bastard, a bit of his own medicine for once;" she sat back smiling to herself as she carefully continued caressing her long, red fingernails with her fine emery board.

#

Beth once again found herself sitting in front of Kate Monroe, knowing that whatever was going to happen, it needed to happen soon. She was in turmoil, unable to sleep or eat properly, unable to think about the new school term which was only days away, unable to share this huge problem with anyone and she had never felt more alone.

"So, Beth, have you had a chance to speak to your parents about this? Have you made any decisions?"

"No, no. I can't speak to my parents, they'll go mental. I just feel trapped, but I guess the only thing I can do is get rid of it; I have no other choice, do I?" Beth stared at Kate with oceans of worry and fear etched on her face, exhaustion rings under her eyes, fingers tearing at a paper tissue on her lap. Kate was also in well-disguised turmoil, desperately trying to display calm reassurance but agonising over her own mistake all those years before. She felt compelled to alert Beth to the lifelong after-effects she could suffer from an abortion, but knew her relationship with Beth must remain professional, not stray into the personal. What to say, how to protect her, Kate was silent for a few minutes.

"You know Beth, I really should have alerted someone immediately I knew you were pregnant because you were under the legal age of consent and I was worried for your safety; you should have your own social worker assigned by now, but I didn't call anyone because you were so sure you were safe and I believed you. Now you're sixteen, you can have a termination without your parents knowing, but you will need care afterwards, support from someone. Not many people, especially at your tender age, are spared the trauma of a termination without needing some counselling or, at the very least, TLC from someone close."

"Why, why can't I just have the termination and go home afterwards, sleep it off, carry on with life as usual? I have to do this, there's no other way, I can't cope with my parent's reaction to all this if they find out."

"Right, you need to understand the risks, possible side effects. Just as your monthly periods can affect your mood and general wellbeing to a lesser or greater degree, so can an abortion, but much more so." Kate paused, struggling to keep her own personal sense of loss and grief under wraps, trying to separate her own experience from Beth's, but not quite succeeding. "Beth, I had a friend who was in your predicament, only a year or so older than you. Her parents forced her into an abortion, prioritising their own hopes and dreams for their daughter, not considering her opinion; her future prospects were the most important thing, not an unwanted and unplanned child. That poor girl suffered unimaginable pain and discomfort for a couple of weeks, plus guilt, sorrow, emptiness and severe depression long term. There was no counselling, so she went to stay with her grandparents for a few months to recuperate. She eventually went on to have a full career as a…teacher. Years later, when she wanted to start a family of her own, she couldn't. Years of IVF were fruitless, she's childless to this day. You see Beth, it's not a quick fix, something to risk lightly, there's often a big personal price to pay. Yes, some people have two, three or more abortions and suffer very little, but it's not always the case, you could suffer major trauma." Kate sat back in her chair, took a deep breath to compose herself and waited for Beth to respond.

"I have no choice, I have no support, nowhere to turn, please refer me to the abortion clinic; the sooner this is over the better."

"OK, if you're sure there's no-one you can turn to," and Kate picked up the phone to arrange an urgent referral to the gynaecology specialist at the hospital.

#

It was later that day when Molly opened her front door to find Joe standing there, making no effort to welcome him in.

"Hello Mrs Gregson, is Beth home?"

"Yes, she is," came the flat reply devoid of all emotion, which Joe couldn't help but think reflected her perfectly.

"Well, could I see her please?"

"You'd better come in, you can wait in the kitchen while I go and get her;" Joe sat anxiously as he listened to Molly amble unhurriedly up the stairs, wondering if Beth would bother to see him. Molly reappeared some minutes later. "She wants you to go up to her room, you remember where it is, but I insist you leave the door wide open, do you hear?"

"Yes, sure," he instantly replied, wondering exactly what the implications were, whether she knew of Beth's condition and, if so, whether she thought Joe was responsible. His long legs took the stairs three at a time and he soon found Beth sitting miserably on her bed, hugging a pillow closely to her chest.

"Hi, how are you feeling?" he whispered, slowly perching on the end near her feet. She didn't reply, just looked at him sadly. "I……um…...I'm really sorry about the other day, but I was so surprised, shocked really, angry and hurt, I felt as though you'd cheated on me," he tried to explain. Beth stared at him for a long moment before responding.

"Why, why is this all about how *you* feel, how angry *you* are?"

"Because you obviously have a boyfriend or something that you've kept hidden from me Beth. I thought we were best mates, that we shared everything and trusted each other, that we were growing up, growing closer, but I was wrong, clearly."

"What boyfriend, I don't have a boyfriend, you know I don't, other than you," she said, trying unsuccessfully to stay quiet and calm so that her mother couldn't hear her.

"How then, how did this happen? Has someone attacked you, raped you or something? You know you could have told me if anything bad had happened to you, I would have helped you."

"That's just it Joe, I don't know, nothing awful like that has…...it's a nightmare. I've spent the whole summer trying to pretend this is not happening; I couldn't even be honest with myself, how could I be honest with you? I've never had sex, yet I'm pregnant, how can that be?"

"PREGNANT, did you say PREGNANT?" Molly's screech was piercing as she swept into the room. "What have you been up to, dirty little slut. What will people think, what will they say, especially with your father running the type of clinic he does. And you…" she shouted, turning to glare at Joe, "you can get out right now, NOW, do you hear me?" Joe stared her out for a moment, a mixture of shock and disgust for her rising like bile in his throat. He tore his gaze away from her and looked at Beth, now weeping silently into the pillow she was still hugging.

"Beth, do you want me to stay, I will if you need me? And for the record Mrs Gregson," he said, his eyes still firmly fixed sympathetically on Beth, "I'm not the father, but I care enough about Beth to stay right here if she wants me to."

"Get out, I said, GET OUT," came her almost hysterical reply, whilst she grabbed his arm and tried to pull him off the bed.

"Stop, just leave please Joe, I'll call you later," Beth spluttered through her tears, not looking up as he quietly left the room.

"And you," Molly thundered, "what are you planning to do, because I don't want another child in this house."

"You won't," was the tearful mumbled response she heard as she followed Joe down the stairs to make sure he'd left.

#

The latest afternoon presentation at S.K.I.L.L. had gone well and Finn was pleased that they had enrolled twenty more students for the research programme. There had been no more hysterical outbursts like the one they had experienced that first afternoon, though it had now become predictable that a handful of students would reject the proposal without further discussion. Ray was thrilled that they now had over one hundred students ready to put the research into action, just as soon as the new academic term got under way.

Ray opened his front door to an unusually quiet house – no sounds coming from the kitchen, no juicy aromas to indicate dinner was under way, just a strange sense that something was out of the ordinary.

"Hello, anyone home?" he called, but nothing came back.

"I'll go up and have a quick shower, freshen up, leave you to find out what's going on, ok?" said Finn as he headed upstairs. Ray found Molly horizontal on the sofa, eyes closed and a small icepack on her forehead. She didn't stir, just waved him away with one hand.

"What's going on, are you ill?"

"I have a migraine. Beth's.....Beth's....... staying in her room tonight and I'm not hungry. You'll have to take Finn out for dinner, that's all."

"Oh, ok, but....is anything wrong, this is unlike you?"

"I just have a migraine Ray. We need to talk later, but not now, not with him needing dinner, so just go out. I'll be fine." Ray paused outside Beth's room on his way up to change; he tapped on her door and opened it just wide enough to peep in and see her sitting up with her face buried in the pillow she was still hugging, exactly as she'd been just hours earlier with Joe and her mum.

"Everything ok Beth?" he enquired? Her red-rimmed eyes looked up and stared blankly at him.

"I suppose she's told you so go on, say what you want, you can't make me feel any more miserable than I do already."

"No, mum hasn't told me anything, what do you mean? Quick now, Finn's waiting to go out for dinner, mum says you're staying in your room – tray supper tonight?"

"No, just go, you'll know soon enough and not hungry;" she rolled away from him into a foetal position, clearly ending the conversation. Ray turned and shut the door, finding Finn right behind him as he did so.

"Teenagers eh? Who knows what goes on in their heads?"

"Not me Finn, not me."

#

"I just can't believe how awful that woman is, she's evil," Joe said as he shook his head, still sitting at the kitchen table. His supper remained untouched and sat stone cold on an ancient plate, greasy gravy seeping slowly into a hefty dollop of potato mash. Freddy was at a sleepover and Joe had been describing how upsetting the ordeal with Beth and Molly had been.

"Now Joe, you don't know what sort of life Molly Gregson has experienced to make her that way, don't slip into judging her too harshly." Martha was trying to understand what Molly must be feeling, as well as Beth.

"Mum, Beth's just sixteen and frightened, what sort of mother only cares about 'what people will think' instead of her own daughter?"

"One who hasn't ever been taught better Joe, one who hasn't been shown maternal love herself. Now, try to focus on Beth love, not her mum; what's she going to do?"

"Beth called me a while ago – I don't think she has a choice mum, her mum won't have another child in the house. Beth must get rid of it and then get back to school as if nothing has happened, but how is that even possible? That baby is a full person, half Beth, whoever the father is, how can she be expected to just trash something….some*one* who is half her? She's asked me to go with her ….should I?"

"That's up to your own conscience Joe. She's your dear friend and she needs your support because she has no-one else, but is that all you'd be doing, or would you be helping her to get an abortion? I can't decide that for you Joe, but I won't judge you, whatever you decide." Molly sat quietly with Joe, both deep in thought, before she spoke again. "One thing to consider though Joe – if there's any chance that Beth wants to keep her baby, I know of people who will help her, places where she can get the support her parents aren't willing to give. Talk to her quietly when you get a chance but, by the look of her, she's getting close to the time when a termination ceases to be legal, so sooner rather than later." Martha walked around the table and gave Joe a hug, before she set about clearing the supper dishes away.

#

Finn looked across the restaurant table at Ray, who had been mildly distracted throughout their meal. Celebratory discussions about reaching their goal of one hundred students enrolled in the programme had been subdued, slightly preoccupied as Ray was at the unusual events earlier at home.

"Is Molly ill, Ray?"

"No, I don't think so, just some mother/daughter issue going on, but it feels more serious this time than usual, something I can't put my finger on which has infuriated Molly." Finn considered his next words carefully as he gazed around the crowded restaurant, barely an empty table in the sumptuous and vibrant room.

"Ray, I hope I'm not speaking out of turn, but if I may make a few observations?" He'd decided this was exactly the right time and place to raise this topic, averse as Ray was to any public conflict or confrontation. "I have noticed the last couple of times I've stayed at your place that Beth has avoided alcohol, that her appetite is smaller, that she is sometimes nauseous at rich deserts – that she is gaining a little weight – is it possible that she's…." his voice had dropped to a whisper, …. "pregnant?"

"What? Don't be ridiculous, she's only sixteen," came the instant reply.

"Exactly, she's sixteen, not a child but a young woman, an attractive one at that," Finn replied with a leer to his smile. Should he carry on, or should he stay quiet, he wasn't completely sure but decided to risk it anyway, knowing Ray was not man enough to create a noisy scene. "I hoped my plan had worked, to get our little scheme off to a start, you know what I'm saying? Always best to keep early plans 'close to home' if you get my drift and it seems mine may just have been fruitful, if you'll excuse the pun."

"No, what…what exactly are you saying Finn? Have I got this right, that you …..what…..seduced ….forced yourself on my daughter? Are you insane?" He instantly stood up scraping his chair on the hard floor and heard it crash down behind him. "What, you stole her innocence, in my own home? You absolute bastard, I ought to… ought to…..smash your bloody face in right here, right now." Ray was clearly very agitated, his voice getting dangerously loud, struggling to stay in control, ready to lash out with anger bubbling inside him. People on neighbouring tables turned to look, their conversations instantly disappearing into a general hush throughout the room.

"Calm down Ray, you do want our commercial programme to be successful, don't you? It's not going to happen if you get physical with me, if you make a scene here in this restaurant. What would that do to your reputation Ray, people here know you, don't they?"

"You shit Finn, you absolute shit. What sort of man are you?"

"One who's going to make you very rich, Ray, if you keep a lid on your temper. She didn't suffer, she didn't even know about it, probably still thinks she's a virgin, thanks to my little green friends," he grinned as he patted his breast pocket. "She was bound to be 'broken in' by someone soon anyway, she's an attractive girl; rather a man who knows what he's doing, than some spotty teenager.   Anyway, we can sort her out at the clinic, perfect, as planned. Now, are you going to get a grip and sit down, or are we going to end our partnership right here, right now?" Finn stared at him with the coldest, steeliest expression as he spoke through gritted teeth.

"No, no way, people know me too well, someone might see her going into the clinic, what would that do to my..*our* reputation. But I tell you this Finn, you can stay at a bloody hotel from now on, starting tonight; we'll collect your things from the house, there's a hotel in town. Beyond work we have no contact from now on,

82

understand? You stay right away from Beth and Molly, do you hear? Now get up, we're leaving," and he strode angrily ahead of Finn.

"Don't worry Ray, Molly was never in any danger from me, never," he laughed as he replied.

#

SEPTEMBER

It was a warm late-summer Saturday afternoon as Martha stood outside the local hospital with twelve of her church friends. She turned her face to the soothing caress of the sun as she prayed silently, holding up a banner which shared her message with walking and driving passers-by. The twelve each held a different poster, each one presenting the value of every human life, some offering contact details for anyone in need of help, anyone suffering from abortion in any way, pre or post termination. Financial help, emotional help, physical help, practical help, it was all there for the asking, along with prayers of support.

Occasionally someone would stop and ask what was going on, what was the purpose of these twelve witnesses. They would receive the briefest of quiet information, all of which was present on the posters. It was regular for a passing driver to peep a horn and give a thumbs-up sign, roll down a window and call words of support; it was equally not irregular for a passing driver to do the reverse, to display two fingers and call words of abuse, even aim a spit in the direction of the witnesses. Either way, the response was always the same, a smile, a wave and a 'thank you for your support' reply. On only one occasion had Martha known a full-on verbal attack, only a few weeks earlier. A large van had paused in the hospital exit driveway near the road, a few metres away from Martha. A very angry young woman, anguish etched on her thin face peering out from between mousy, waterfall hair, had rolled down her passenger door window and screamed at Martha:

"You fucking judgemental bitch, who gives you the right to stand there and judge those poor women inside, if you only knew what they were going through. It's not easy for them you know, it's so hard for them, you evil witch.

Why don't you just crawl away and die somewhere."
Martha had been taken by surprise, shocked to the core
and was instinctively feeling attacked and simultaneously
relieved that the woman had remained inside the van, but
she knew she was meant to resist the urge to respond. She
was immediately thinking that those poor babies inside
were suffering a worse fate than their mothers, but it was
no time to argue.

"We're all entitled to our opinion," was all she quietly
said before she turned away, but she later found herself
praying for that poor woman, who was clearly suffering
from painful involvement with an abortion, either directly
or indirectly.

An hour later, Martha noticed two familiar figures
walking towards her, holding hands, heads down. As they
neared her, Martha called out Joe's name gently.

"Mum, I'd forgotten this was one of your witness
days." He stood for a few moments before speaking again.
"I don't know what to say mum, we're just …Beth has an
appointment inside." Beth had not said a word, just stood
silently reading the messages on the twelve posters being
held up along the street. Molly walked up to her and gave
her a big hug, before returning to her spot near the drive.
Beth was suddenly seized by sadness, fear and confusion
and could not take another step.

"Joe I can't, I just can't….. can't walk past your mother
and go in there; I'm scared, I'm really scared," then the
tears began to flow. Joe held her close as he guided her
away down the street and Martha began to pray that may-
be, just may-be, another little life had been saved.

#

"Well, did you get rid of it? Your father's disgusted by the
way," Molly barked, as she stood hands on hips in the
hallway as Beth entered the house.

"Yes," she lied, boldly staring her mother in the eyes as
Joe stepped in behind her.

"You needn't think you're coming in here, you've done enough damage already haven't you?" Molly put a hand up to block Joe's entrance.

"Mrs Gregson I …."

"Mum! Joe is not responsible, you've been told that, so please let him pass. I don't want any supper either, I'm going to Joe's." The two of them went up to Beth's room, leaving Molly speechless at the foot of the stairs, open-mouthed at her daughter's defiance.

"Why did you tell her you'd had the termination when you haven't?" Joe whispered once her bedroom door was shut.

"I don't feel strong enough for the shouting which would have followed if I'd told the truth Joe. What on earth shall I do now?" The look of utter desperation on Beth's face almost brought tears to Joe's eyes, but he just wrapped her in a bear hug and stroked her hair gently.

"Shush, don't get upset; we'll have a quiet talk with my mum tonight after Freddy's in bed, I'm sure she'll come up with some practical suggestions, so don't worry." Joe instantly wondered why he'd placed such a huge responsibility on his mum's shoulders, without her even knowing, whilst he rocked Beth back and forth for a few moments.

#

Unusually for a Saturday, Ray drove back to the office, having met Finn for an awkward breakfast meeting at his hotel. Ray had wanted to make sure their partnership still existed, he couldn't afford to lose it, but he'd also wanted to ensure Finn was securely back on his flight to Switzerland, without the risk of him coming anywhere near the house or Beth. His concern for his daughter weighed on him, but he'd put too much time, effort and money into this new venture to risk losing it; this was their livelihood, their standard of living at steak, plus Molly had assured him that Beth was booked in for a termination that very day, so the problem was only temporary, wasn't it? Therefore, no need to front up to either of them about who had got Beth into her current situation; better not to risk any emotional reaction which might jeopardise the success of his business contract with Finn and their future income. Finn would not stay at the house again in future, Ray had made that clear, so things at home should be back to normal within a week or so, he was sure of it.

Once in the office, he'd send a quick e-mail to Finn affirming present student data for the start of the new academic year only a week away, then he'd collect Molly's perfume from his desk drawer; their anniversary was still a week away, but an early gift might cheer her up a little and he definitely didn't want a moody, difficult wife all weekend, that was certain.

#

Martha's sitting room was so cosy that her toes were almost touching Joe and Beth's as they sat opposite her on the sofa, all three sipping huge mugs of steaming, comforting cocoa. Molly knew she'd help Beth if she could, but she also needed to protect Joe, make sure he didn't try to be the big hero.

"Well, I'd be lying if I said I wasn't thrilled that you still have your baby Beth, but I know that doesn't solve your problem. Knowing how things are at home love, I'm sure you're hoping I have some ideas of the way forward and we can talk about that shortly, but first, how did your parents react?"

"They don't know, they think I went through with it."

"Do you not think they'll notice your growing tummy? Won't secrecy make it worse long term?"

"In two weeks it'll be too late to force me into an abortion, so their fury will die down I hope, they'll have no choice but to accept the situation. Until then, I'll carry on wearing loose clothes, keep a low profile – they don't want to be in my company right now anyway." Beth sounded lost, but Molly was impressed by her unexpected decisiveness.

"OK, let's look at your options then love; I have some details and contacts that you can consider which will help you through your pregnancy, then your baby will have a good chance at life, even if you decide to put him or her up for adoption." Molly went off to get her SPUC folder, as Joe squeezed Beth's hand in reassurance.

#

Kate and Wilf were busily sloshing a vibrant, terracotta emulsion paint on the walls of their new hobby room, opposite the one starkly white wall they'd painted the previous weekend, having removed all evidence of it's would-be-nursery existence. Kate was singing along contentedly to an Abba song on the radio when thoughts of Beth invaded her consciousness. Wilf was immediately aware of her change in mood, concerned that she may be regretting their decision to abandon all hopes of a baby.

"You ok love? Feel like a cuppa and a biscuit break?"

"Yep, just as soon as we've finished this wall, almost there so can't stop now."

"Penny for them then, 'cos you've abandoned Abba mid-Waterloo and disappeared into your own head," Wilf said, as he leaned in with a grin to plop a small spot of terracotta paint on her nose.

"Oi, what are you doing?" she yelped as she stepped back, a smile reaching the corners of her mouth and eyes.

"Nothing, just love you, that's all. So, what are you thinking about?"

"Actually, I was just thinking about Beth Gregson, wondering if she'd had her termination yet, I know it's scheduled."

"It's Saturday Kate, she has a designated social worker guiding her and she's not your responsibility right now, so stop worrying. Come and have a cuppa, we've got

Hobnobs too, come on," then he took the roller from her hand and led her downstairs towards the kitchen.

"I still care though Wilf, that's all, can't help it."

"I know and that's because you're a wonderful doctor and a wonderful person. Now, I bet you can't eat three Hobnobs."

"Bet I can, before you get two mugs of tea on the table too. Let's go shopping for wetsuits later and sign up for those sailing lessons we've been promising ourselves, then we'll have something to put in our hobby room," she replied, cramming the first biscuit into her mouth.

#

Ray arrived home late afternoon, carrying an enormous and expensive mixed bunch of flowers for Molly, as well as the perfume stashed in his briefcase. He'd also spent an hour selecting a pair of diamond stud earrings for her and he felt he'd made a huge effort for his wife this year, usually delegating the purchase of gifts to Sophie. He knew he'd taken Molly for granted a lot lately; she was also angry and distressed about Beth's situation and how it would reflect on them as parents, so she needed pampering a bit today. He'd take her out to dinner as well, to her favourite French restaurant, which would hopefully distract her somewhat and lighten her mood.

"Hello Molly," he called as he entered the house, "anyone home?"

"In the lounge, drinking wine," came her slightly slurred voice. "There's a bottle on the table in the kitchen if you want some." Ray pondered his next few moves and decided to put the flowers in a vase in the kitchen, where they'd be discovered shortly, then give her the other gifts at the restaurant later.

"Beth not home then?" he asked.

"No, she's gone to Joe's for supper thank goodness, I just don't want to look at her today. You look pleased with yourself...why?"

"No reason. I'll get a glass of wine and join you, but don't drink too much as we're going out to your favourite restaurant later, all booked for 7.30pm. I thought we'd celebrate our anniversary a few days early, the last week has been so difficult for us both," and he disappeared back to the kitchen.

#

OCTOBER

The new school year was well under way and, fortunately for Beth, she was now a sixth former and no longer bound by school uniform; this would eventually make it far easier to disguise her growing tummy under over-sized sweatshirts or check cowboy shirts. Joe had chosen science subjects for his A-levels whereas Beth was doing languages for her three subjects, so their lessons were no longer shared, but they still met before and after school as much as their timetables allowed. Though Beth was at her happiest in Joe's company or at his cosy home with Martha and Freddy, she did however have to go back home each evening, whether she wanted to or not.

#

Molly was in the kitchen, chopping vegetables for dinner, when Beth walked in to get a drink. It was a warm late October afternoon, so Beth was just wearing shorts and a loose T-shirt, loose enough not to cling to her body but also sheer enough not to disguise her shape if the sunlight was behind her – it was!

"Beth, you're still overweight, which I can't understand when it's now six weeks since your termination. You really must stop eating rubbish, because you look as though you're still pregnant."

"I am," was all Beth said. The opportunity to inform her parents just popped up, so she took it instinctively.

"You are what?"

"Pregnant, I'm still pregnant," she said almost defiantly, as she turned to face her mother.

"What? No, you had a termination, you told me you did," came the shrill, fearful reply.

"No, I told you I had an appointment for one. I didn't go through with it. So, no, I'm not eating rubbish, it's all baby," she said, laying her hands gently on her rounded belly.

"You stupid girl, what were you thinking? What about school, your plans, your future? What about us, your father and me? What will people say? That we can't even sort our own daughter out?"

"What do you mean, 'sort me out?' I'm not a problem to be solved."

"You are in this condition. We could have sorted this out quickly and efficiently at S.K.I.L.L. if you'd had the sense to tell us in time. Your father's job, our life, we'll be the laughing stock of the town if our own sixteen-year-old daughter can't even be sorted out by us. You really are so selfish and thoughtless Beth, I can't believe this." Molly's tone was getting louder, higher, more hysterical with every syllable.

"Mum, I don't understand. S.K.I.L.L. is a research centre, how could dad 'sort me out' as you put it? What do you mean?"

"Dad's business isn't just a research facility, Beth. What do you think is used for this research? Foetuses, that's what. It's an abortion clinic and dad could have made this problem go away if you'd told us when you first knew you were pregnant."

"I don't believe you – an abortion clinic? Our home, our food and clothes are funded by abortions? That's terrible, just terrible, I never realised."

"Don't be so naïve Beth, it's all perfectly legal and normal, but how does it look when our own teenage daughter, *you*, are in this condition? How does that reflect on your father and me?"

"Is that all you care about, how you and dad *look*? Why aren't you concerned that our whole lives are based on the death of babies?"

"Oh, for goodness sake, you've been spending too much time with Joe and his 'holier-than-thou' mother. I forbid you to go there any more, *no more*, do you hear me?"

"You can't forbid me to go anywhere and you can't force me to have an abortion either, it's too late now, I'm thirty-one weeks gone." Molly instantly stepped towards Beth and slapped her face hard, shocked by her own actions for a moment.

"You selfish little …. what about us? I do not want another baby in this house. I *will not* allow it. You'll have to go somewhere else to have it and get it adopted, but it's *not* coming here."

"Incredible, this baby is half me mum, one quarter you and you're just burying your head in the sand, rejecting it and me? I don't know why you even had me. I bet you wish you'd terminated me too, don't you?"

"I…I…don't be ridiculous…I…"

"Don't bother, I won't shame you any more mother, sorry to have been such a bloody disappointment to you." Beth left the room distraught, tears rolling down her blotchy face, unable to handle the hurt and rejection. She wondered what sort of mother *she* would turn out to be …just like her own mother? No, for the first time since this all began, Beth suddenly realised how much she now wanted her baby, how protective she finally felt towards it, now that they were both facing overwhelming rejection. At last, her mother had unwittingly done something to help her in all this, by waking up some buried loyalty to the life growing inside her. She would not reject her baby, she was now determined.

Martha and her pro-life friends had decided to extend their silent prayer vigils outside the hospital, to include being present outside other abortion clinics one day each month. Today was their first day outside S.K.I.L.L. and the dozen or so friends were unsure of the reaction they'd receive from passers-by. They had acquired police permission to hold their vigils, but the first time at a new location was always a little un-nerving. They'd been silently standing for half an hour, holding up their posters and banners, when Ray Gregson emerged from the building with a tall, blond man beside him. He immediately met Martha's gaze and approached her, menace etched on his face.

"What exactly are you lot doing here? This is private property and you are causing a distraction to the people entering the clinic for treatment."

"Good morning Mr Gregson. Actually, we're on the public pavement and we are causing nothing, just standing silently with our posters."

"Your posters are in complete conflict with the ethos of the S.K.I.L.L. clinic, implying that we are other than a research facility, so please remove yourselves before I ask the police to remove you." Martha shook her head at his description of the clinic.

"This is a peaceful witness to the value of life; we are not noisy or threatening, just silent, plus we have police permission to be here. I suggest it is you who are causing the distraction, not us," Martha replied, barely louder than a whisper.

"I've asked you to leave, so will you do so immediately please," more of a command than a request. Martha placed a single finger to her lips, implying 'quiet,' then shook her head gently. "Right, I'm calling the police. You'll learn you can't defy me so publicly and you can tell your damn fool son not to appear at our house again too." Back in the office within moments, Ray stormed past Sophie and barked orders at her even more aggressively than usual. "Get the police on the phone for me, *now*!" Sophie knew better than to do anything but obey his gruff instructions and dialled immediately. Several minutes later she heard an extremely angry Ray slam the phone down and rage at Finn, who had been two steps behind him as he both left and returned to the office. "Damn and blast the useless police force we have in this country. They can't even move some wet woman and her band of loonies when they are causing a disruption to businesses. Hopeless idiots." Ray had to accept that his demands were being ignored and admitting defeat on this occasion did nothing for his mood; Sophie knew she'd bear the brunt of it eventually - she didn't have to wait long.

"Sophie, why didn't you tell me those halfwits were outside when they first arrived, before they first set up camp. We won't tolerate this sort of disruption to our customers."

"I didn't realise they were outside Mr Gregson, or I would have told you."

"It's your job to look after the smooth running of this clinic Sophie – if I can see out of the window then so can you, stupid girl. I don't know why I bother to pay you at the end of each month – I might have to review that if you don't smarten up your performance." An hour later, the group of friends concluded their vigil with a prayer and went home peacefully, having seen no more of Ray Gregson or any police.

Sophie had had enough of being on the receiving end of Ray's temper outbursts. She decided there and then to accept the position she'd been offered at the pilates studio and began to type up her resignation letter as soon as Ray returned to his office. Yes, she'd compose and print her letter on his computer and his printer and also on his time, serve him right. In the meantime, his precious chocolate biscuits were in for a hammering.

Joe was surprised after dinner that night to learn where his mother had been earlier in the day.

"But mum, Beth's dad's clinic is a research centre for long-term illnesses isn't it? Why would you stand there?"

"Joe, they use aborted foetuses to do their stem cell research; they have been an abortion centre for over two years, the research is a new venture according to his secretary Sophie, who goes to the same pilates classes as I do. She told me they're recruiting students and paying them, to increase the number of foetuses they have access to, specifically for research programmes. No doubt there's a financial gain to be had long-term for the Gregsons too. I doubt Beth knows all this, or she'd have mentioned it at some point I would think."

"I'm shocked, what a dark and horrible way to earn a living, poor Beth – no wonder they're so furious about her pregnancy. I need to think about this, it's awful," then he was gone from the table.

By early November Kate had seen Beth several times at the pre-natal clinic and was happy that all was progressing normally. Weekly visits were due to begin very soon, for the final stretch of Beth's pregnancy.

It had been a long and busy day at the surgery when a very pale young girl walked in to see Kate and it was clear she was in a weakened state.

"Come and sit down, what can I do for you?"

"I'm bleeding heavily, it just won't stop. It's been going on for a few days now and I feel really ill."

"Are your periods usually heavy at the start and how long do they usually last?"

"No, never like this and they're usually over with in four days."

"Have you recently altered your sexual behaviour, had any coil or IUD inserted, anything different from usual?"

"Yes, I have. I have a new sex partner; I was pregnant and I had a termination, all since September."

"So, you and your boyfriend decided on a termination – where? At the hospital?"

"I don't have a boyfriend, just a sex partner. This was the start of our involvement with research into life threatening illnesses, at the S.K.I.L.L. clinic – I had the abortion there."

"I'm not sure I understand how you are involved in research, can you explain?"

"It's a student sponsorship programme, which helps to avoid long-term bank loans in exchange for participating in the research."

"Ah, so you had the termination at the clinic. Why didn't you return there immediately you felt unwell?"

"There's no option to do so. If I have problems, then I'll be taken off the sponsorship and I can't afford to do that, so I came and registered here."

"You mean you are paid to get pregnant and then have a termination, is that what you're saying?" The girl nodded.

"OK, let's have a look at you."

After a brief but informative examination, Kate feared the girl's prospects of future motherhood could be as remote as her own and wasted no time calling for an ambulance. An hour later, the girl was lying in a hospital bed on a drip, having intra-venous antibiotics for a severe uterine infection, as well as suffering from dehydration and damage to her womb.

Before leaving for home that night, Kate called for an early morning meeting with the other GPs at her surgery. A serious breach of medical practice required immediate action.

Beth was stretched out on her bed with her headphones in her ears, listening to her favourite downloaded music, when Molly marched into the room without knocking. The headphones were quickly pulled out.

"You are beginning to look obviously pregnant Beth and I just won't have it, people noticing and talking about us. This is going to affect your father's reputation and I told you I won't have another child in this house. I've decided that you can take a break from school for the rest of this term – we'll see if the school will let you resume studies in January, after you've had it…got rid of it, got it adopted, whatever. You'll have to go and stay with grandmother in Gloucester until then, I'm sure we can persuade her – we may have to pay her though, so that will be your allowance gone."

"What? I'm not going anywhere, especially to grandmother's – she's never shown any interest in me at all and I haven't seen her since I was about ten. I'll wear looser clothes or something, hide my bump better."

"No, not good enough. If you won't go to her you'll have to see if granny Gregson in Lincoln will let you stay, but *you* can explain *why* to her yourself. Anyway, your father and I are going away for Christmas, three weeks in the sun somewhere and you can't come – you won't be allowed on a plane that late in your pregnancy; so, you'll have to go somewhere – you can't say here alone. You got yourself into this mess, you sort it," then she left the room leaving the door wide open. Beth lay still and quiet for a few minutes, struggling to take in the conversation they'd just had – her mother would actually get on a plane and leave, without giving her daughter a second thought …… she was speechless, unable to process this latest rejection.

"Can you believe it mum, the Gregsons are actually going away for Christmas and leaving Beth behind – they simply don't care about their own daughter. She's heavily pregnant and they're just burying their heads in the sand, completely washing their hands of the whole situation."

Martha could see that Joe needed her to say something, but she wasn't quite sure what; she didn't want to judge Beth's parents, however disgracefully she thought they were failing their daughter, yet she couldn't bring herself to excuse them either. Instead, she just reached out and held Joe's hand for a few moments.

"You know mum, I've been wondering what sort of a horrible family this baby will be born into, poor Beth. I've actually been thinking that may-be we got it wrong and it would have been better for Beth to have had a termination after all." Well, that was a statement Martha had no problem arguing against and she was quick to respond.

"Joe don't ever think that. Every poor little soul deserves a chance at life and no-one's ever responsible for the family they're born into, so why should they be punished for it? Better to be adopted into a family who'd love them and make them feel wanted."

"This baby is just going to experience rejection, like Beth, so isn't it better to be out of it?" He wasn't sure he really believed this, but he needed convincing.

"Joe, do you know that, since the 1967 Abortion Bill was introduced by David Steel MP, about 9,000,000 babies have lost their lives in this country alone? How can that be right? How can that be legal? It terrifies me that we live in a society where so many so-called 'civilised' women can kill their own children Joe. It's not possible that *so* many women are physically, emotionally or mentally so ill that they can't proceed with their pregnancy, yet that was the main criteria originally, supposedly verified by two doctors each time. No, it's become just another form of birth control, with a total lack of acknowledgement that each and every termination ends a human life, deprives another human of their right to choose for themselves what sort of life they'll lead. If a mother wants to chop off her own arm or leg that's fine – your limbs are 100% your own body, but an unborn baby has an individual heart, lungs, everything, independently of its mother, despite being inside her, and life can be sustained outside the womb from as little as 22 weeks gestation now." Joe could see how passionately his mum felt about this topic and truly realised, for the first time, why she did all the things she did, said the things she said.

"I didn't know all this mum, tell me more," and he moved closer on the sofa to put his arm reassuringly around her shoulder.

"I get really upset about the way the world is going with this Joe, that's all. You know, there's an MP in London right now who's presented a Bill in the ten-minute hearing slot twice in Parliament, supporting the complete decriminalisation of abortion. It was defeated the first time around but has now been successful, which means she'll be working to present it for a full hearing in Parliament soon. If passed, abortion will be legal right up to full term Joe and that's only a step away from what America has approved in numerous states, New York being the latest – abortion actually during labour. As long as a child is still inside its mother a doctor can legally crush its skull and pull it out of the mother limb by limb - how is that not murder Joe, legalised murder? It's terrifying. What sort of society are we turning into? You can have legal charges brought against you for kicking a dog, hitting someone, or even swallowing a live goldfish at a fete, which was in the news recently, yet you'll be able to end a fully developed human child's life legally – it just doesn't make sense. People have become desensitised because it happens every minute, every day somewhere, they've accepted it as normal, but they'll be loud and vocal if they see animals in poor conditions, neglected or treated without respect, like battery hens or six-month-old lambs going to the slaughter houses. How does society see infanticide as fine and animal cruelty as appalling? My God, the agony those poor babies must feel!" Martha was openly weeping now and realised she was being comforted by Joe, when it should have been the other way around. Then she decided it was not a bad thing for him to see how strongly she felt, because if parents don't teach their children that abortion is wrong, then the world will teach them it's right.

"Mum, you've convinced me, I'm with you on this OK. Now, dry your eyes and I'll make us both a hot cuppa – I don't know why a cuppa is always the answer, but it is," and off he went to the kitchen. As he pottered around with mugs and milk he knew he'd have to be strong for Beth, because she had no-one else.

#

Kate, the practice manager and the three GP partners sat around a table very early the next morning, professional concern etched on all their faces. They had devoured two croissants each and several cups of powerful 'wake-you-up' Kenyan coffee from the cafetière Kate had brought in for the occasion (believing 'instant' was inadequate for such an important discussion), leaving a multitude of crumbs all over the melamine table-top and a strong caffeine-infused aroma in the relatively small conference room at the rear of the surgery.

Kate was the senior partner in her practice but, at their early morning meeting they had all agreed, with surprise and disgust, that the S.K.I.L.L. clinic was breaching the ethical codes of practice that all GPs in the country were expected to adhere to and that, more than that, they were potentially and knowingly endangering the health of the students they were enlisting for the so-called 'research programme.' As a result of the hour-long discussion and whilst still in their presence, Kate lost no time in contacting the three doctors in the area, often nicknamed "the three wise men," who were appointed by the Area Health Authority to keep an eye on colleagues who may be having difficulties of one sort or another. She also knew that, with the information she was giving them and the evidence of the poor girl now lying on a hospital bed on a drip and recovering from a dangerous vaginal infection, "the three wise men" would waste no time in taking action and reporting the S.K.I.L.L. clinic to the General Medical Council, who would investigate and eventually hold an emergency hearing; with the strong possibility that the S.K.I.L.L. Ethical Committee would be found to be approving the practises operating outside the law, the clinic would undoubtedly have its license to continue in practise revoked.

Kate was also aware, as she composed her letter, that she was almost certainly making Beth Gregson's life somewhat more difficult and she felt it her duty to speak with Beth before the day was out. With that in mind, she later left Beth an urgent message on her mobile asking her to pop in after surgery the next day, at the same time reassuring her that there was nothing to worry about regarding the baby, that it was another matter altogether.

#

"Hello, hello, gran is that you?" Beth was trying her best to stifle her tears, but her voice was broken by her efforts to swallow them down. She was curled up on her bed, her door tightly closed against her mothers prying, hugging her pillow close to her chest for comfort, as she often did.

"Beth, is that you love? You sound strange, is everything alright?"

"No, it's not gran, I…I…I have a big favour to ask you – can I please come and stay with you for a while?"

"How do you mean love, do you mean mum and dad too, or just you?"

"Just me gran, alone. For Christmas and may-be a bit longer, what do you think?"

"Well, I suppose that would be fine Beth, but why just you? Aren't you spending Christmas with your mum and dad?"

"No, they're going away for a few weeks and I can't go with them gran."

"Why ever not Beth? I don't understand, but of course I'd love to see you darling." She could already feel the warmth and security of her grandmother's voice wrapping itself around her down the phoneline, offering her some sense of hope that had deserted her for so long.

"They're flying abroad and I'm not allowed to fly because....because.... I'm 35 weeks pregnant gran, I'm so sorry." With those words her strength faltered and all that could be heard down the phone were great gulping sobs.

"Beth love, why didn't you call me before now? What's going on?"

"I...I... couldn't..." and no more words would come to her.

"Right, now listen to me Beth. Firstly, calm down a bit, of course you can come to stay, for as long as you need to. I'm guessing your mother is not thrilled at the situation, so I'll call her tonight to discuss things, but how she....they can just fly off and leave you...I'm stunned. Never mind, we'll have a good Christmas together with grandpa, so stop crying love. You just think about when you want to come and how you plan to get here, remembering grandpa doesn't drive any more, then we'll make our plans Beth, OK?

"Yes, thank you gran, I love you and I'm so sorry to... to... I don't know."

#

Martha put a large cottage pie and a bowl of broccoli in the middle of the table and watched as Joe dished a portion up on to Beth's plate. It had become fairly regular to have a fourth plate on the table, even when Jack was away, but Martha was happy that Beth clearly felt relaxed and happy in their home.

"Mum, Beth has decided to go and stay with her grandmother for a while in Lincoln and she's travelling up there on the coach before Christmas. She's not really happy about travelling so far alone when she'll be about 36 weeks pregnant, so I've said I'll go with her just to make sure she's safe, then I'll come home again. Is that OK with you? You'll be alright for a day or so without me?"

"Joe, that's a great idea, of course she can't travel that far alone, but you'll need to come straight back because her grandma won't be expecting to have you to stay too. When exactly are you both planning to travel?"

Joe looked at Beth with a questioning look on his face.

"Beth?"

"Oh… yes… in about a week to ten days, I haven't confirmed it with gran yet. She's happy for me to stay on too, until after the baby's born, then we'll decide what to do after that. I just don't know what will happen, don't know how I'll feel…it's so hard."

"What about your commitments here Beth, your social worker and doctor's visits and so on?" Martha was concerned that Beth was properly prepared for the difficult weeks ahead.

"My social worker knows and is pleased I'll be getting the support I should have had all along, from my parents. I'm seeing Dr Monroe tomorrow and I'll tell her I will register with Gran's doctor as soon as I arrive in Lincoln – Gran's already asked at her surgery if I can do that." She smiled weakly then, but her smile looked anything but confident to Martha, who had nothing but concern and respect for this brave young woman.

"Are you alright...... financially..... Beth, or do you need help? I can give you a little if you need it?"

"No, thank you, I'm fine. I've been saving my allowance now for six months, plus my parents will pay for my coach fare and a bit more, as long as they don't have to confront all this. I've applied for various benefits too, which I'll receive in due course. Thank you though, that was kind of you."

"Well ok, but you just tell Joe if you find you're a bit short and we'll see what we can do, alright?" Beth nodded and smiled again, unable to speak for the lump in her throat at such generosity, compared to her own parents.

#

The next evening, Ray slammed the front door in fury as he marched into the kitchen, where Molly was stirring a pot of something meaty on the Aga.

"Do you know what that blasted interfering woman Kate Monroe has done? She's reported me for malpractice and S.K.I.L.L. is now facing a formal investigation by the Regional Deanery Ethical Committee – can you believe it? First that stupid Lehman woman outside the clinic with her bunch of religious cronies, now this. Why can't people just mind their own bloody business and let us all get on with our jobs – I wouldn't be surprised if they know each other and they've planned this together." He grabbed a wine glass from the cupboard and slammed a bottle of wine down hard on the table, making Molly jump.

"Well, you haven't done anything wrong have you, so what can they possibly find? It's not going to stop us going away for Christmas, is it?"

"Is that all you care about? This is our livelihood Molly and it could all be at risk?"

"Why, what have you done Ray? Why is our livelihood at risk, what do you mean?"

"Nothing, just stretched the rules a bit here and there that's all, but they won't like it. As if we didn't have enough on our plates right now with Beth messing our lives up, I just don't need this, that's all." He poured himself a large glass of red wine and glugged down three great gulps before topping it up. Molly stared, wondering if she was going to get a glass before it was all gone."

#

"Come in Beth, it's good to see you, how are you feeling?" Kate was relieved to see that Beth was somehow calmer than she had been on previous visits, almost peaceful.

"I'm fine thanks, just feel heavy, that's all."

"Ah yes, very normal in the last weeks of pregnancy. Let's have a look at your weight, listen to baby and check your blood pressure then." Beth was now used to the routine, accustomed to hearing the rapid heartbeat of the baby, familiar with having her ever-increasing baby-bump examined and tolerant of the uncomfortable tightness of the blood-pressure cuff.

"Well, all seems to be spot on Beth, a very neat pregnancy. Come and sit down for a minute - how are things at home? Are you getting on ok with your social worker?"

"Yes, all fine and I've applied for the benefits available to me too, she's been really helpful. Actually, I'm going to stay with my grandmother for a while and I wondered if you could let her GP have my details, once I've registered?"

"Of course, as long as you register immediately you arrive …. where? You'll need weekly checks once you reach 36 weeks gestation, OK."

"Lincoln. I'll be staying for a while, until I decide what to do, after the birth I mean."

"Good, so you'll be going fairly soon then won't you – it's important to be away from unnecessary stresses in late pregnancy, but I'm sure you know that already. Well, I hope the next weeks and months go well for you Beth, be sure to come in as soon as you get back, won't you?"

"I will and thank you doctor, you've been a real support to me. Was there anything else – you called me?"

"No, no, just wanted to check you were getting organised because – well, you're very young and you've had a difficult few months at home, that's all." Kate smiled at this girl who'd been so brave, stronger than she herself had been in the face of pressure from her own parents all those years before. Beth smiled and left the room, whilst Kate was left hoping and praying that Beth would already have left town before the next turbulent chapter in the Gregson house erupted.

#

"Sophie, what the hell is this all about? You can't resign with immediate effect, you have to work a month's notice. Why now anyway?"

Ray was red-faced with anger at this latest unforeseen bump in the road and would happily vent his fury at her as was usual, if he didn't need her so much. He stood menacingly over her desk, staring intimidatingly down at her, trying to impose an authority he felt was rapidly escaping him. For once Sophie was not fazed by him.

"Actually Mr Gregson, I can. I know my contract states a month's notice but, if you remember, I've taken no holiday this year yet because we were extra busy setting up the student programme – you couldn't spare me. That means I'm owed four weeks paid leave which I'll take starting next Monday, because I start my new job at the pilates studio in two weeks and I need a short break before then." The satisfaction that she felt at this situation and his discomfort was not evident in her poker-face expression, but the glow inside was doing wonders for her self-respect – this moment was long overdue.

"But you can't, that gives me no time to replace you, you selfish girl. Who's going to run the clinic? If you want a reference, you'll stay long enough to replace you."

"I can and I will Mr Gregson, I know my legal rights; the clinic is no longer my problem once Friday arrives. Also, you might want to work on your attitude if you want your next secretary to stay longer than five minutes, plus I don't need a reference because my cousin runs the pilates studio. Now, if there's nothing else tonight I'm going, because it's already ten past six. Goodnight." She was gone in a flash of red fingernails and strong perfume, leaving Ray with a rather nauseous sensation in his throat, staring into her now vacant seat.

#

Kate arrived home to find Wilf in the back garden, not in the kitchen sorting out supper, as was usual. He was sitting in their twin hammock chair with a steaming cuppa in his hand, not the glass of wine he usually preferred in the early evening, swamped in a thick sweater against the late autumn chill at dusk.

"What, not eating tonight then?" she teased as she sat beside him.

"Yes, I've booked us a table at the pub down the road, didn't feel like cooking tonight. There's still tea in the pot if you want one."

"No, I'll wait for wine thanks. I'm tired and could do with distracting from a challenging day, so going out is good."

"Tell me what's happened today then."

"Well, I've been summoned by the Deanery Ethical Committee – I have to discuss in detail with them the reasons I reported S.K.I.L.L., who the student I sent to hospital was, all I know about the student recruitment set-up and so on, all the details."

"Wow, well you knew that would come – you're not regretting opening up that can of worms are you, I know you better than that."

"No, of course not, but it could get unpleasant and I'm now beginning to wonder if Beth was a reluctant victim in all that, but I believed her insistence of her total innocence Wilf. I just don't want to cause her any more grief, so I won't mention her if I don't have to, I just hope that's the right thing to do – I already stretched my own professional position by not reporting her to social services immediately she first came to me."

"Well, you can't change the past and you'll have to be honest about her if her name comes up ….she is the Gregson's daughter after all, so it's entirely possible she's implicated and, as she was only fifteen when she first came to you, perhaps you should make a point of mentioning her, cover your own back, as it were. "

"Yes, of course …….what a messy business life can be sometimes."

"Come on," he said as he patted her knee, "the pub won't hold our table forever, let's go." Five minutes later they were walking down the road together holding hands.

#

DECEMBER

Ray and Molly were travelling at 35,000 feet above France when an e-mail message popped up on his open lap-top; it was from Finn, a curt and business-like text informing Ray that their professional involvement had been terminated and funds withdrawn. No further contact would be possible, Finn's company would admit no liability nor accept any responsibility for the unethical practices employed at S.K.I.L.L., because Ray had signed a waiver releasing them from culpability at the start of their business relationship, in exchange for a higher percentage of the spoils when the research was completed and actual treatment for various illnesses was launched world- wide. Greed had been his downfall and he would have to face the consequences alone, whatever they turned out to be – he would not know until January at the earliest.

It was vital that Molly didn't see this particular e-mail, if Ray wanted to have any sort of peace whilst they were away and, right now, he just wanted to hide from the chaos surrounding the clinic. He'd sent an e-mail to all students on the programme informing them that research had been temporarily suspended, so no more sponsorship funds would be transferred to them until further notice – anyone who currently found themselves pregnant should contact a family planning clinic for advice and 'treatment.'

Luckily for Ray, Molly was preoccupied with her in-flight magazine and the large glass of red wine in her hand, whilst waiting for her lunch to arrive, happily oblivious of the troubles which would catch up with her lifestyle in the months ahead. Thoughts of Beth couldn't have been further from her consciousness, confident as she was that her daughter was on her way to her grandmothers for a while, where the baby problem would be dealt with.

"Don't you just love flying off somewhere warm Ray, it's absolute bliss to leave it all behind," she said without looking up from her magazine.

"Yes, glorious," he said, as he shut down his laptop firmly, pushing any anxieties to the back of his mind for now.

#

At that exact moment, Martha was dropping Joe and Beth off at Exeter bus station, ten minutes before they were due to board a coach for Lincoln. It was going to be a long journey, over nine and a half hours with a change and an hour long wait at Bristol, but at least Beth wouldn't have to struggle alone with her heavy suitcase. They were both a little apprehensive of the long day ahead of them, but they were happy enough to be travelling together. It would not be a particularly comfortable experience for Beth, sitting for so many hours in a restricted space with her now quite large baby bump; the advice from Kate had been that she stand and stretch her legs every thirty minutes, walk to the toilet at the rear of the coach and keep her circulation moving, to avoid any risk of DVTs, so she'd set her mobile to ring at half-hourly intervals as a reminder. With a substantial picnic-type lunch packed by Martha in their bags, sweets, bottles of water and numerous downloaded games apps on their phones, they happily settled into their seats near the front of the coach for the start of their journey. As they pulled out of the coach station they saw Martha standing on the curb waving happily, her smiling face concealing the instinctive concern she was feeling inside, maintaining the waving until the coach disappeared from sight in the busy traffic.

#

Kate had been sitting in front of the Regional Deanery Ethical Committee for over an hour, discussing all she knew about the practises which had been going on at the S.K.I.L.L. clinic. She'd delivered her verbal and written report on the student who had suffered such awful post-termination complications, as well as the knowledge she'd received from her that she was out of danger and recovering at her parent's home. Her future prospects of parenthood could not be guaranteed, but that would be determined in due course, as had Kate's own disappointing experience.

As Kate left the RDEC office she passed Sophie in the corridor, who had also been summoned to give evidence of all she knew. Although Kate did not know Sophie, she recognised that her presence must indicate that she was employed at the clinic in some capacity and nodded politely as they passed each other.

Sophie had been assured that she was not implicated in any illegal practices, especially as she had now left the clinic, although her timing was a fortunate coincidence rather than a bout of conscience about the student recruitment. The evidence supplied by Sophie was invaluable, as she'd been at the clinic throughout the period of time in question, had set up and organised the student programme under instruction from Ray and had witnessed students coming and going for their preliminary health checks and terminations. She had also been astute enough to print and save some copies of incriminating leaflets and signed 'waivers' by students, for her own insurance, knowing that it would only be a matter of time before she left the clinic because of the rude way in which she had always been treated. Ray's days were definitely numbered, she was sure.

#

The wait at Bristol had been pleasant enough for Beth and Joe, relieved as they were to leave the coach and have a welcome stroll along the length of the indoor station. They smiled at the large Christmas tree next to a newspaper stand, where two small children were hopping up and down excitedly. There was also a street piano at one side of the walkway, where a young man was happily plonking out a George Esra song and singing along with a surprisingly good voice.

They wandered up to the far end of the station and visited the toilets, before sitting at a small café and enjoying a hot chocolate and a doughnut. Time passed quickly and they were on their coach to Lincoln before they knew it, happy to be looking forward to the next stage for Beth at her grandparents, rather than back at the nightmare she'd left behind. Christmas was only a week away and happy thoughts were beginning to occupy Beth's brain, knowing she had some small gifts for her grandparents in her bag as well as a small white bunny for her baby; yes, she was feeling positive for the first time in a very long time.

#

The box of decorations was sitting on the floor in the middle of the Lehman's small living room whilst Jack, who was home for a whole fortnight this year, was making sure that the real tree Martha had insisted on buying was secure in its oversized pot. Freddy was getting impatient, knowing that the tree lights would have to be put on first, but he especially wanted the decorations he'd made at school to have pride of place – Rudolph and Santa, made out of clay and now as hard as rock, brightly coloured and fired in the school kiln a week before.

"I wish Joe was here, he always does the decorations with me, he's really good at it," Freddy complained as he hopped up and down excitedly in front of the tree.

"He'll be back before you know it, so just enjoy doing it your way for once. Where do you want to put Santa and Rudolph?" Jack tried to distract him, but he and Martha both knew they'd be happier when Joe was back home safely, able to be a kid again instead of the responsible adult role he'd assumed of late.

Martha had told Joe to come straight back home the next day, once he'd delivered Beth safely to her grandparents, so she could adjust quickly to her new if temporary home; but he'd bought an 'open return' ticket, just in case of emergencies, so there was always the possibility he'd be away longer than planned. Still, he was sixteen after all and would possibly be leaving for university in a couple of years, so they'd all have to get used to being without him for longer periods eventually. Hey ho, so hard when your kids grow up, she thought as she reached for the Christmas tree lights and passed them to Jack, who was now standing on a small ladder.

#

Apart from being on call for a night or two on the out-of-hours NHS 111 emergency phone line, Kate also had a full two weeks away from work over the Christmas and New Year holiday period. It had been a stressful time at work lately, what with her RDEC meetings regarding the S.K.I.L.L. clinic complaints she'd made and the usual heavy influx of sick people at this time of year, afraid they wouldn't get appointments and repeat prescriptions until the middle of January. Kate was exhausted and Wilf had tried unsuccessfully to persuade her to take a break abroad, but she knew she should be on hand to give any further evidence the RDEC might ask her for. She was determined that Ray Gregson would not escape the professional crimes he had committed.

No, she was happy to hunker down in their cosy home over Christmas, well stocked as they were with the ingredients for Wilf's marvellous recipes, their favourite wine and the company of her sister and brother-in-law for a few days. Home and life couldn't be better, she thought happily as they snuggled in front of a roaring log fire a few days before Christmas. As she stared at the flames, she couldn't help privately wondering how Beth was though, but she said nothing and kept those thoughts tucked away in the back of her head.

#

Granny Gregson opened the door to Beth and Joe, immediately pleased to see them, but clearly something was not quite right.

"Oh dear Beth love, I've been trying to call you on your mobile, but you didn't answer. I've been calling your parents too, but I expect they're airborne by now, aren't they?"

"Yes, mum and dad left early this morning, before we did. What is it Gran, what's the matter?"

"It's Grandpa, he's had a nasty turn and he's been taken to hospital in an ambulance. They think it's a small heart attack or stroke, but they're not sure. I have to go, but I was waiting for you to arrive; I didn't want the pair of you locked out. There's a ham salad for you in the fridge, fresh bread in the bread-bin, just help yourselves darling and I'll be back as soon as I can – my neighbour is waiting to take me in his car, as soon as you arrived."

"Do you want us to come with you Gran?"

"No love, you settle in here; you know which room is yours and Joe can have the sofa bed in the lounge. I'll call you as soon as I know what's happening." A quick hug for Beth and Joe and she was gone in a blue Corsa. Beth went to the bathroom whilst Joe carried their bags into the cosy cottage and then slumped heavily on to the sofa, tiredness suddenly catching up with him. He woke up two hours later to find Beth snoozing quietly beside him, then decided it was way time he let his parents know they'd arrived and that he might not be home quite as soon as he planned.

#

Jack was none too pleased that Joe may be away longer than anticipated and began to really question why Joe was carrying so much responsibility, when he wasn't the father of Beth's baby.

"You know Martha, I'm away from home so much with work, trying to keep you and the boys in house and home, I'm rather annoyed that Joe's disappeared almost as soon as I arrived. Now it's possible he might be in Lincoln for the whole of Christmas – why?"

"Jack, Beth's been totally let down by her parents, her only support has come from Joe and us, plus her doctor of course. Her parents have swanned off in an aeroplane somewhere hot, leaving her to cope when she's only a few weeks off her delivery date – incredible. Neither Joe nor I felt we could let her travel all that way to her grandparents in Lincoln on her own love, she's too vulnerable." Martha knew where this conversation was going and she didn't want to overreact, she wanted him to accept the situation for what it was. Jack was getting into his stride though and allowed his annoyance to lead the way.

"I really don't know why she didn't have a termination; she's sixteen, her whole life is ahead of her, her studies etc, do you not think her parents may have been right Martha? Her future is being sacrificed for the sake of a small mistake that thousands of young girls make, why not deal with it and move on?" Joe knew Martha's strong opinion and her faith would not agree with his words, but he was angry his son had left so quickly and his Christmas was being disrupted by a family he barely knew.

"Jack, I don't want to argue at Christmas, but you know how I feel about abortion and I'm proud of Joe and his support of Beth. However that baby was conceived, *it* is innocent of any wrongdoing, so why should it just be eliminated without a second thought? This way it will be loved by someone somewhere, it will have a chance at life."

"OK," he said, "I know how you feel and I can't imagine a life without our boys, so I'm glad you stood firm seventeen years ago when I suggested a termination. You must admit though, it's commonplace now, almost not worth discussion, like having your teeth out or something."

"It's not Jack, every termination is a life lost and you know it. Discussions are going on all over the world; opinions are changing, rights and health issues are being fought out in court all over the place, it's such an emotive subject. Did you know that in America, governors of numerous states have signed bills in recent months banning abortions once a foetal heartbeat is detectable, at around six weeks gestation, unless there is rape or incest involved and sometimes not even then? Georgia, Alabama, Kentucky, Mississippi and Ohio, they're all signed up to the 'heartbeat bill,' but people are protesting that women's rights are being stripped from them and they're challenging the proposed bills in the federal courts. At the same time, people in this country want to completely decriminalise abortion, as they have in New York, which is terrifying. Where America leads, we usually follow not far behind, so I hope and pray that decriminalisation here gets defeated in government and that the 'heartbeat bill' gets introduced here eventually. Now, I don't want to discuss this any further tonight and I'm going to make us some tea before bed, so I suggest you catch up with the late night news or something to distract your thoughts," then she disappeared before Jack could say another word.

#

Beth and Joe had been sitting at the hospital bedside for two hours, staring alternately at her grandmother's worried face and her grandfather's heart monitor bleeping repetitively whilst he slept.

"Beth, I can't leave him love, I must stay beside him; we haven't had one night apart in fifty-two years, you do understand, don't you?"

Beth nodded and smiled her understanding, but sadness prevented her from responding immediately. Joe was quick to read her mood and spoke before she had a chance to.

"You mustn't worry about Beth Mrs Gregson, I won't leave her whilst you're needed here – my parents understand the situation. I've got enough clothes for a couple of days, then I'll need to use your washing machine though, unless I'm going to stink you all out." He laughed at his own humour, trying to lighten the mood, but they both just smiled.

"You're a good boy Joe, I can see how much you care about Beth, but please just call me 'gran' won't you?"

"Deal," he said, happy that he could ease a little of her worries. "I'll get you something to eat and drink from the café before Beth and I leave, give you a few moments together, OK?" Gran smiled and gave him a big hug and a £10 note, then he was gone.

#

At exactly the same time, many miles away, Sophie was in a restaurant celebrating her new job with her cousin and a few friends, regaling them with memories of the awful criticisms Ray had levelled at her over the previous two years of her employment at S.K.I.L.L. They were astounded, not only at the rudeness he dished out to her, but that she had remained for as long as she did. She reminded them that she had not only been paid well, but that she had also regularly enjoyed his expensive chocolate biscuits as well as 'christened' them for his next visit to the biscuit box and had also enjoyed his wife's perfume, which had them laughing hysterically.

Meanwhile, Kate and Wilf were sitting in front of their log fire, a favourite habit of theirs, this time wrapping Christmas presents together whilst enjoying a new bottle of Chablis, prior to their guests arriving the next day. They'd made a promise to each other that all talk of their respective jobs was taboo for the entire holiday season, though Kate knew she'd regularly wonder how Beth was progressing and how the hoo-ha over the S.K.I.L.L. clinic would erupt in a couple of weeks. For now though, she was happy to keep all such thoughts to herself.

Not too far away, Jack and Martha were showing Freddie photographs of previous Christmases, when he and Joe had been little and had demolished not only the tree, but also all the chocolate decorations hanging on it – on more than one occasion. Freddie loved this, it sort of compensated for Joe not being with them for the first time ever.

On a different continent entirely, Molly and Ray were waking up in a very hot bedroom, the noisy air conditioning ensuring that they didn't sleep in late each day. Molly toyed with the idea of phoning Lincoln to check that all was OK, but may-be she'd just leave it for another day or two; no news was good news wasn't it and no doubt they'd have been contacted if there had been a problem – they *had* actually left their contact details, hadn't they? Ray was in the shower, so she'd remember to ask him after breakfast, no rush.

#

Seven days later Joe and Beth were still living at her grandparents whilst they themselves remained at the hospital. Gran slept at her husband's side each night on a lazy-boy chair, unwilling to leave him even though he was in gentle recovery from his stroke. She was confident that Joe was taking good care of Beth, but she still felt uncomfortable that she wasn't home with her granddaughter herself, especially considering how close the expected birth date was getting.

It was Christmas Eve and the three of them had enjoyed a hot meal in the hospital restaurant before walking back to Grandpa's single room. He smiled at them as he watched them place a few small wrapped gifts on his bedside table, then they sat and enjoyed the distant sound of some carol singers who were in a ward down the corridor. At nine o'clock Beth and Joe were asked by a nurse to leave, which they did after big hugs and kisses from Gran.

It had been snowing heavily for a couple of days and, by the time they left the hospital, the snow was deep and crunchy under their feet.

"Let's walk Joe, it's such a bright and beautiful night and I feel like some fresh air after the stuffy hospital."

"OK, but hold my hand in case you slip, we don't need you in hospital tonight too."

They momentarily wondered where her parents were, but they'd had no contact apart from two text messages. There'd been no cards or gifts from them, just a hefty bank transfer into Beth's account the week before with instructions to buy something nice for her grandparents.

Joe had spoken to his parents every day since he'd left, but they'd reassured him that all was fine at home and his place was definitely with Beth whilst she needed him, so he felt no guilt about being away from them and Freddy. They missed him but they were proud of him.

As they walked down through Broadgate they could see a massive church ahead of them, a flickering glow gently shining out through the massive, arched stained-glass window above the doors. It looked warm and inviting and, after walking for half an hour, their fingers and feet were cold.

"What's that light coming from the church Joe?"

"It's candle-light I think, there must be a Christmas Eve service going on inside. Shall we go in for a bit, warm up before we walk the last mile home?"

"Yes, I'm frozen and it would be nice to get some of that Christmassy feeling – it's such a contrast to last Christmas at home."

As soon as they entered the church, Joe realised it was midnight mass, so familiar to him. The main church lights were off and every person was holding a candle, singing carols along with the church choir. Joe felt homesick for the first time and wondered if his family was also in church right then.

The hymn sheet told them they were in St. Hugh's church, a huge stone building with strong pillars down each side of the central aisle. A large Christmas tree covered with tiny white lights glittered to the right of the altar and a small make-shift stable was to the left, housing all the main characters of the story apart from one, where the manger lay empty.

"Joe it's beautiful, I've never seen anything like this before – my parents have never been church-goers. Can we stay for a while, or should we leave?"

"We can stay if you really want to, it's so warm in here, but don't get too cosy because we still have to walk a fair distance afterwards."

"No problem," she smiled, "I feel great and more alive than I have done for days."

An hour later, having sat through the carol service and midnight mass, Joe and Beth watched as dozens of people wished each other a happy Christmas, hugged, shook hands, collected up hymn books and blew out their candles once a few subtle corner lights were switched on in the church. How so many strangers could be so kind to each other was a surprise to Beth but, as she watched, she realised they were not really strangers but probably saw each other regularly. As they themselves stood to leave, Beth was suddenly aware of a gush of warm water escaping down her legs inside her jeans. She promptly sat down again.

"Joe, I need to just sit here for a moment, OK?"

"Why, what's the matter? Are you alright?" She was an essentially private person and the thought of causing some scene here amongst strangers horrified her, so she'd wait until they had all left before she made a move. Just then she noticed a small room to her left, unoccupied and dark.

"What do you think that room is Joe?"

"I think it's the confessional, where people go to discuss things privately with the priest."

"Can we go in there and have a look?"

"Well, I suppose so, but there's nothing in there except a chair usually." No-one noticed them slip quietly into the small room and Beth sat down after closing the door gently behind her.

"What are we doing in here Beth?"

"I want the church to be empty before we leave Joe, because I think I've just wet myself. My bladder is so unreliable lately, it's embarrassing."

"OK, we'll give it ten minutes, then I'll peep out."

Ten minutes later they were alarmed to discover that, not only was the church empty, but it was locked and dark, except for a soft light at the front near the altar. As Beth gave the big door a last hard push, she felt what seemed like a flood of warm water inside her clothes and she realised with shock that she must be in early labour.

"Oh no Joe, I need to sit down again, I really do, my waters have gone." She quickly headed back to the comfort and warmth of the small room, folded her thick scarf and plonked it on the chair to mop up any surplus fluid escaping from her and sat waiting, wondering what to do, trying to calm her nerves whilst Joe tried all the other doors. Her pulse was racing and her hands were shaking, but she had no power to stop her body following its own course, all she could do was sit it out for now.

"It's no good Beth, all the doors are locked and the windows too high, plus my phone has no signal Beth and everyone's gone home, what the hell are we going to do? I think we may be here for the night. Labour can go on for ages, mum told me, let's hope she's right; the priest will be back for an early morning service, so all we can do is stay warm in here until then, OK? We'll have to ask him to call for a taxi or something then, alright?"

Beth noticed that he was at least as anxious as she was at that moment, panic stricken really but trying hard to hide it, but they really had no choice but to stay put. She comforted herself in the knowledge that she'd seen a recording of a birth at one of her pre-natal classes so, all being well, she had an idea of what to expect. With luck, things could go slowly until morning.

#

At five-thirty on Christmas morning the parish priest sat bolt upright in bed, wondering what had woken him when he'd only had four hours asleep. He was tired but awake and puzzling this when he heard the unmistakeable sound of a baby crying.

"I must be dreaming, I just need to go back to sleep," he said to himself as he lay back down on his pillow and shut his eyes, but there it was again, a definite wail of a hungry baby. He got up, pulled on his dressing gown and went downstairs to investigate, when he realised the sound was coming from inside the church.

The end

Useful contact details:

Government benefits available to pregnant teenagers:

There are programs available for pregnant **mothers** and expecting **teens** through government **assistance** like Supplemental Nutrition **Assistance** Program (SNAP), Infants, and Children (WIC), Children's Health Insurance Program (CHIP), Temporary **Assistance** for Needy Families (TANF), and Medicaid.4 Dec 2017

- <u>Family Lives</u> – visit the website or call 0808 800 2222 for support for families, including young parents
- <u>Family Nurse Partnership</u> – a family nurse may be able to visit your home, if you're young parents, to support you from early pregnancy until your child is 2
- <u>Shelter</u> – a national housing charity that can advise you about housing options and housing benefits for young parents; visit their website or call them on 0808 800 4444

Pregnancy birth & baby:

- <u>Additional Child Care Subsidy</u> (transition to work)(commonly known as JET Child Care Fee Assistance) — to help pay for child care if you want to start working again or are job searching, working or studying
- <u>Family Tax Benefit</u> (often called the 'small pay') — to assist with costs of raising children
- <u>Parenting Payment</u> (often called the 'big pay') – the main income support payment to assist with costs of raising children

- <u>Household assistance</u> payments — for example, Single Income Family Supplement and the Energy Supplement

Contact Centrelink 3 months prior to birth on Families and Parents Line: 13 61 50

Pro-life organisations offering counselling and care:
- Good Counsel Network: 020 7723 1740
- Image: 0161 273 8090
- Life: 080 802 5433

Practical Help For Students:
- Alma Mater Fund: 07849 088244

ARCH – Abortion Recovery Care Help - counselling & support post-abortion.

International Adoption Guide: 4 Antrobus Road, London W4 5HY

St Francis' Children's Society: 48 Newport Road, Woolstone, Milton Keynes. MK15 0AA   01908 572700

Adopters for Adoption: 0800 5877 791

IAC – The Centre for Adoption: 22 Union Street, Barnet, London. EN5 4HZ 020 8449 2562

Acknowledgements

My husband, Ian, for believing in me as a writer and for having such a positive response to the first draft.

My daughters Debra and Sara for their brutal honesty as proof readers, both brave and confident young women.

My granddaughter Robyn, for alerting me to current 'young person' language.

My ex-GP and altogether great doctor, Mark Hedges, for overseeing medical correctness.

Brave and honest friends Jan Taylor, Clare Lawrence and Jesse Lawrence, for excellent proof-reading and for not being scared to tell me where I'd made errors.

Society for the Protection of Unborn Children (SPUC) for their continued efforts to win the pro-life/pro-choice battle, also for allowing me to use two prayer vigil images.

DISCUSSION QUESTIONS

- What are the major differences between Beth and Joe's home lives?

- At what point do you think Kate realises her own experience is clouding her judgement?

- Is Sophie's revenge strategy on Ray justified?

- Do you think Molly is afraid of her husband?

- Why do you think Beth is unwilling to hold Joe's hand, preferring to carry books?

- Is Joe justified in feeling hurt when he realises Beth is pregnant?

- Why do you think Ray is so weak in Finn's company?

- Why do you think Finn said to Ray that Molly was in no danger from him?

- What effect on Joe has his father's long-term absence had?

- Who would you turn to if you were in Beth's situation?

- Has your understanding of abortion been altered by Beth's story?

- Has your opinion about abortion changed by Beth's story?

Lightning Source UK Ltd.
Milton Keynes UK
UKHW010635180321
380569UK00001B/192